Ottakar's LOCAL HISTORY *Series*

Walsall

The Bull Stake in the 1960s. The Victorian buildings can be seen still intact.

Ottakar's LOCAL HISTORY *Series*

Walsall

Pippa Bradley

Rushall Square, showing the clock and drinking fountains in the late 1900s. Picture provided by Rachael Sheldon.

First published 2002

Tempus Publishing Limited
The Mill, Brimscombe Port,
Stroud, Gloucestershire, GL5 2QG

British Library Cataloguing in Publication Data.
A catalogue record for this book is available from the British Library.

ISBN 0 7524 2671 0

Typesetting and origination by Tempus Publishing Limited
Printed in Great Britain by Midway Colour Print, Wiltshire

Contents

Acknowledgements

First of all I must thank everyone who sent in an entry to the competition. The response was overwhelming and the standard of entry very high. Deciding which submissions to leave out was almost impossible and took a great deal of painful deliberation! Unfortunately however, there was only so much space.

Thanks are also due to Dr Carl Chinn who was kind enough to give me air time on his radio show on Radio WM. Thanks also to Jane Markham who allowed me to talk about the project on her show on Saga Radio.

The book would never have come to fruition had it not been for those establishments and organisations who helped to distribute leaflets and offered advice on whom to contact, namely the Local History Centre, the Leather Museum, the Art Gallery, the Walsall library and the *Walsall Observer.*

My thanks also to George Mann, manager of Ottakar's in Walsall for all his support. Finally I would like to extend my gratitude to Claire, Denise, Dean, Dom, Aimee, Helena, Sonya and Tim, who covered for me with good grace while I disappeared into the office on numerous occasions to work on the editing of the book.

Introduction

There is a wealth of books and articles produced by historians on aspects of Black Country life, such as chain and lock making, metalworking, the leather industry, limestone working or coal mining. Yet talking to people about their own memories of life in the area is equally fascinating and often gives a totally different angle on the everyday realities rather than just the well recorded events of local history.

I hope you enjoy reading about the experiences, memories and research of the people who have so kindly contributed to this book. In choosing the pieces, I have tried to include a variety of approaches and styles, illustrated whenever possible with photographs, drawings and cartoons which themselves provide a unique record of Walsall life.

Pippa Bradley, August 2002.

1 Memories of the Locality

Webster Road and the sandhole

Having acquired No. 78 Webster Road in 1929, my parents, along with other families, set about landscaping their gardens and taking pride in their new council houses. Almost every family had children and there was no shortage of playing space. In fact, the area was a paradise for small children by virtue of a disused sandpit, which in fact was owned by C.C. Walker Ltd of Marlow Street who employed about 100 workers. He was also a local town councillor and became mayor of Walsall in 1903 and 1905. He was always referred to by local people as 'Coddy'. This sandpit of very high quality building sand was situated off Ryecroft Lane. It was adjacent to the Walsall to Cannock LNWR, which later became the LMS railway line, and to some boundary posts in a line from Essex Street to the Midland Railway bridge that carried Ryecroft Lane over the Midland Railway. This ran from Water Orton to Wolverhampton. Local senior citizens can recall the sandpit in use, and the land that Webster Road was built on was then used for cattle grazing. In the 1920s most of it was acquired for allotments. In the 1920s and then the Depression years, almost every householder rented an allotment to grow food for the family. When the sandpit was working it was a magnet for children from Essex Street and Ryecroft. Mr 'Coddy' Walker did not take kindly to this practice and often called the police to move these children, who in return regarded him as a killjoy. Many years later, when these children were grown up and having children of their own, they were surprised when Coddy Walker left the sandpit land in his will to Walsall Council to be made into a permanent playground with swings and roundabouts for children.

There was an attempt to fill in the sandpit with household refuse in 1936. As it happened it coincided with a very hot summer, causing the residents of Essex Street and Webster Road much discomfort as millions of flies invaded our households and several children went down with diphtheria, scarlet fever and stomach upsets. Even North Walsall school was not immune from the plague of flies, despite being some 100 yards away from the sandpit. It was both comical and annoying to see many flypapers hanging from each household and classroom ceiling (fly sprays and repellents did not exist at this time). Flypaper consisted of a liquid glue that attracted flies by scent. When the fly landed on the hanging paper it promptly got stuck. In trying to become unstuck it buzzed its wings until it was exhausted and died. If one was taking a nap in a chair on a hot summer's afternoon the noise from these trapped flies was considerable. Some did, however, find the strength to escape but usually fell exhausted onto the dinner table. These flypapers were hung from the lightshade situated in the centre of the living room. As it was customary in those days for the dining table also to be in a central position, mealtimes were often interrupted by a dying fly falling into one's dinner. Many flies chose to spend their last moments of life in the sugar basin since they always seemed to be attracted to sugar. The main culprits were larger flies known as bluebottles which could make a lot more noise than the ordinary housefly.

The local shopkeepers sold many flycatchers at 2d each and were often running out of stock. We children used to have a competition to see who could kill the most flies, which when caught were placed in a matchbox. The favourite method of killing a fly consisted of rolling up a newspaper tightly and then flattening the flies as they landed on the table or wall. A stationary fly on the ceiling could be killed by hurling a cork mat with the flat palm of the hand at great speed upwards, thus flattening the fly on the ceiling. It could then be scraped off into our matchboxes. Our mothers did not take kindly to this sport.

Just before the Second World War the tip was full and was levelled off with hardcore and all traces of sand were obliterated. The sandpit became known as the sandhole and today it is always called that, although there is no trace of sand.

Some of the children's games played on the sandhole at times got out of hand. Often a fracas would develop between the Ryecroft gangs and the Essex Street and Webster Road gangs. The preferred method of warfare was hurling stones at one another until sheer weight of numbers caused one gang to retreat. One of our defences was to purloin dustbin lids (made of steel in those days) and use them as improvised shields. Our parents soon noticed dents galore in the dustbin lids and put a stop to our barbaric games. After dark the sandpit took on a new form of recreation – accommodating courting couples. After the pictures turned out at about 10.30 p.m. most couples chose to walk home to North Walsall. During summer months before the refuse tipping, many varieties of butterfly and moth were in evidence. Even after the tipping stopped there was always plenty of insect life along with many species of wild flowers.

Across the sandhole were two pathways – one to Webster Road and one to Essex Street from the former LNWR bridge. These paths were made by the never-ending procession of railwaymen passing to and from duty at Ryecroft steam engine sheds in Mill Lane. Their main problem was the pre-war dense fogs, which were very common before the advent of smokeless zones and clean air acts. Many railwaymen became lost in the pea soup conditions and have been known to spend some considerable time wandering about in circles.

During the 1950s the sandhole became a football pitch for the nearby Coalpool Tavern, who played in the Walsall Amateur Football League. Goal posts were erected and the pitch became a magnet to all budding young footballers. During the light nights of spring and early summer, schoolchildren and teenagers, having finished work, (yes, all teenagers had a job in the 1950s and '60s) would want a game of football and with so many wanting to play it was not uncommon to see twenty a side. The football pitch was eventually buried under tons of soil surplus to requirements during the construction of the M6 motorway in the mid 1960s. The area was grassed and in 1970 it was landscaped with a helter-skelter, roundabouts and children's swings – some fifty years after Mr Walker gave the land to be used as a children's playground. In 1982 many trees were planted to make it an attractive recreation area. Meanwhile on the adjacent ex-Midland Railway land just off Essex Street, a new school for North Walsall infants was built in 1981, a most attractive setting in this part of Ryecroft (vandals permitting).

The strange thing today is that this area is completely devoid of any trace of sand but it is still known to locals as the Sandhole. This includes young people who have no recollection or knowledge of the busy sandpit that provided building sand for many of Walsall's roads and buildings at about the turn of the century.

Jack Haddock

An oasis of green calm known as Mill Lane

The borough of Walsall holds many pockets of woodland, wildlife and open countryside. Places once alive with machinery and industry have now reverted to their former, natural state. Some have remained virtually unaltered over time like Rough Wood, which once formed part of the Royal Hunting Forest of Cannock.

However, many of the open spaces and nature reserves which we love and use today, to walk the dog or just to enjoy nature on display, are very different places to those once busy, loud and often dangerous ones that employed our ancestors over 100 years ago. Iron foundries, brick works, quarries, mines and railway tracks once occupied such tranquil oases which exist amid an equally busy urban setting.

Mill Lane in the Butts is a very good example of this. Situated just over half a mile (1 km) north of Walsall town centre, the present nature reserve has been used and developed over centuries and has played an important role in Walsall's history, and the story has not yet ended by any means. Now under the management of Walsall Countryside Services, Walsall MBC, the area of land which straddles the lane forms an almost triangular shape, with the Ford Brook flowing down along the eastern boundary. Ford Brook has always been an important feature in the area, not only a water supply to local industry around the time of the Industrial Revolution, but also once providing a nucleus for new settlers to live around its banks. One notable settler to the immediate area was a Saxon corn miller named Wagga.

It seems that a mill has nearly always stood at the side of Ford Brook on the edge of the present Mill Lane and although Walsall was never mentioned in the Doomsday Book of 1086, Rushall was entered at this time with acknowledgement of a mill. The mill that once stood in this area was a water-powered corn mill and changed hands many times

View across Mill Lane.

before it fell into disrepair and faded into insignificance. Growers of corn came from far around to have their produce ground into flour. The mill was last used as such during the mid-eighteenth century when William Flower was the last occupier and worker of the mill. In 1883 an iron and brass foundry occupied the site. Eventually the old mill site was owned by the Walsall Electrical Company Limited, who produced electrical appliances including ammeters and voltmeters, as well as outdoor watertight sockets. Also, part of the brook was used as a rope walk by Hawley's Saddlery and Camping Company, who owned many walks within the town, turning rope to be added to nose bags and tents.

The geology of the area surrounding Mill Lane Nature Reserve consists of coal measures, limestone, ironstone (iron ore), sand and gravel. Therefore such resources were exploited fully (although only a few mineshafts may be located around the edges of the nature reserve in particular, on the site that is now Ryecroft Cemetery). During the mining periods between 1831-1851 the population of Ryecroft and the Butts grew from approximately 700 to 2,700, primarily mining families. Although Walsall was host to some extremely heavy mining, it seems that Mill Lane has always managed to miss concentrated mining activity. It is believed that when mining occurred on the site, it only took place on a small scale, perhaps even only in bell pits.

Along the northern boundary of the nature reserve it is possible to access Ryecroft Cemetery, which was opened for its first registered burial in 1894.

I cannot go further without mentioning Ryecroft Junction. This is perhaps what the present nature reserve is best known for, as many local men were employed as firemen, turntable operators, engineers, signalmen and office workers. Morale was high at Ryecroft Junction and for a long time the offices and engine shed complex was affectionately known as 'The Happy Shed'. The junction was responsible for three lines travelling south into town and to Birmingham and Dudley, and four lines travelling north to Wolverhampton, Cannock, South Staffordshire and Sutton. The lines were established between 1849 and 1879. Only two lines are now active, however, and it is still possible to hear freight trains, although they are not visible from any part of the reserve. This must be quite a change from the dirty and noisy working conditions that were experienced daily by junction workers.

During the Grouping Act of 1923, all lines at Ryecroft Junction became owned and managed under the London Midland and Scotland Railway (LMS) and since then locals have always fondly remembered the south side of the junction as the LMS, sometimes contorted by children to sound like the 'Yellow' or 'Yella Mess'!

There was a turntable at Ryecroft Junction which was situated next to the sheds, and was close to the road as it rises to meet the railway bridge. The first turntable was installed in 1878, when the sheds were built. However, the apparatus was small and was manually operated. When turning an engine on the turntable, it was extremely important to centre the engine to ensure an efficient manoeuvre. In 1936, due to modifications at the Junction, the turntable was converted to a larger steam-powered model. This was a lot more efficient and was powered by fixing a pipe from the turntable to the engine, thus establishing a steam vacuum.

A level crossing was in place where the old South Staffordshire line ran past the gates of Ryecroft cemetery, and a small cottage could be found just across the line. This was the cottage of Mr and Mrs Oswin. The couple were employed to open the cemetery gates to let funeral hearses pass through. When Mr Oswin died his wife continued his work until the cottage was deemed dilapidated and Mrs Oswin was relocated to a dwelling with an

Dismantled railway lines.

indoor toilet and hot and cold running water. Adjacent to the cottage was a metal footbridge where many a courting couple would seek solitude. The 'Sixty steps' were so-called because there were thirty steps up and thirty steps down. Remnants of the girders may still be seen under a rough area of bramble.

On the south side of the nature reserve on the site of Ryecroft sheds, an area of high ground may be seen, fondly known by a variety of names: the Alps, Knobs and Monkey Hills. It is a curious formation and although it may have been added to with mining spoil and waste from the time of railway excavations, it seems that the high point existed prior to this. During the Second World War, an air-raid shelter was dug into the ridge in order to protect staff members during the raids.

Over the road, just at the entrance to Mill Lane Nature Reserve, there was even a dog pound, which arrived during the late 1960s and would take in stray dogs. The pound disappeared as late as 1983 and there is now a car park where the building once stood. In 1991 the land comprising the reserve was subject to a land reclamation scheme. Two large pools were created, footpaths constructed and many trees planted which have now formed areas of woodlands. The wildlife value of the reserve is great and because of the naturally acidic, dark soils that are to be found all over the area, and because of the presence of limestone railway embankments, a rich and diverse patchwork of nature has established itself.

This really is remarkable and rather ironic when considering the activity that has taken place on this site over so many years. When walking around the site, as perhaps Wagga did when he first settled here over a thousand years ago, many species of plants and animals can be enjoyed. These include orchids, bladder campion, birch and oak trees, ox-eye daisies, sedges, vetches, many different grasses and insects, including the sallow moth, the ringlet butterfly (which is in national decline) and locally rare fungus *tricloma cingulatum*. Precisely because of the number of species that thrive there in a number of habitats – heath, grassland, marsh, open water and woodland – Mill Lane Nature Reserve is classified a site of local importance for nature conservation.

The reserve is really an oasis of calm within a bustling urban setting. Who would have known that some rare and declining species of flora and fauna would have seen fit to live where once freight and passenger trains hurtled past on a regular basis?

Lucy Martin

Gas lamps and lucky bags – a Leamore childhood

Prize-winning entry

I would like to take you back to an age not so long ago. To a time when a hat-trick for the Saddlers and a hundred with the bat for England still gave you enough time to nip to the corner shop before lunch. To an age where you could cross the 'Rockies' shops, raft the 'Blue Lagoon', explore the 'Jungle' and still be home for tea. A cinema up the road (the Rosum), a chip shop around the corner and steam trains thundering past at the bottom of the street – what more could you ask for? Yes, Leamore was a great place to be growing up in the 1950s and early '60s.

I was born on 27 September 1950, at No. 22 Bagnall Street, the second of three brothers. Older brother Alan, some nineteen years my senior, was seriously wounded in the Korean War and still lives in Bagnall Street with sister-in-law Jean. Younger brother David (two years my junior) now occupies the family home of No. 22.

Dad, Frank (Nank) Till was a no-nonsense miner born in 1908 'down the Sneyd'. The front door of the cottage in which he was born, No. 73 Sneyd Lane, served as our entry gate at No. 22 for donkey's years. The numberplate from the door is still in use on my stable door into the front room of my house in Beatrice Street, Leamore, a great memento of the old days. Granny and granddad Till, Austin, Tom, Ernie, Alice and Elsie made up 'Nanks' family.

Mom, Helen (Nell), was a Humphries, born in 1913 near Little Bloxwich school. She actually taught the younger children while still a pupil there herself. Higher education beckoned but money was a problem, and sadly Nell never got her chance. Granny Humphries, Rose, Anne, Hazel, Sheila, Ben, Jack and Walter made up mom's family. Walter was tragically run down and killed in a blackout during the Second World War, by an Oxo wagon of all things. With most of my aunts and uncles living in Blakenall, Goscote and Bloxwich, we really were a close family.

With the war still fresh in most people's memory the 'Grow Your Own' policy seemed to be the norm. At No. 22 we grew everything from potatoes to gooseberries: you name it, we grew it. Rhubarb was my favourite, cut from the garden, and dipped in sugar; belting stuff. Organic food by the bucketful, helped along by Hooper's horses of Bloxwich. Mr Hooper, the baker, delivered his bread by horse and cart, a nice two-wheeled contraption and, if the horse obliged, it was out with the bucket and spade.

With mom being such a good cook and the garden yielding plenty, 'belting snap' was always on the table. Sunday was the highlight of the week. Breakfast, dinner and tea all had to be eaten. Onions, cucumber and tomato steeped in vinegar, pikelets toasted on the coal fire with a home-made wire toasting fork,

Aunt Clem and Cousin Ted with four-legged friend 'Chum' in Bagnail Street.

snow on the ground outside, *Sing Something Simple* on the radio: teatime bliss.

'Fannies' chip shop round the corner in Providence Street (now part of Leamore flats) was the venue for Saturday dinnertime; proper chips that somehow got nibbled at on the way back. 'What is this hole in the bottom of the wrapper, Colin?' mom would ask after I delivered the family fare. 'Nothing to do with me, mom, Fannie's paper must be a bit dodgy.'

We no longer kept pigs, but the chickens made up for that. Being a miner, dad was a serious pigeon flier. The bottom third of what was a long garden was pigeon city. We had three magnificent lofts all built by Nank himself, fronted by the best piece of lawn you have ever seen. It was well out of bounds to footballing youngsters!

With the mining job went the coal allowance. The Coal Board would drop your coal in the street. You would then barrow it round the back to the coal shed, in this case our old Anderson shelter, untested by German bombers but standing firm as a coal shed and general store. What a great sight it was seeing that same coal burning brightly in the fireplace ('S' hole) on many a winter's morning.

The street contained forty houses with a mission hall at the top end. It was lined by sycamores (now sadly gone) and lit by gas lamps. Not only were these great to swing on, they made cracking goal posts and floodlights, football and cricket being a religion to us youngsters in those days. Day and night, rain or shine, sleet or snow, you were out in the street with a ball of some description. Cars down your road were a rare sight in the fifties, and if one happened to interrupt your game of footie or a Test Match you were really put out! Opposite No. 22 was a goalpost, sorry, gas lamp. In between was a 4ft high privet hedgez above Mrs Jackson's wall, that butted up to her other goal post, sorry, gatepost. This was in football terms a 'net' and a half. The Laundry End of street football, as anyone who's followed the Saddlers will understand.

You didn't have much in those days so you made do and made your own fun: kick the can, red apple, ipstick-I-boo-cherry, statues, hide and seek, marbles and conkers. Small beer by today's standards but the computer games of our time.

John Simkiss (Stunna), Bobby Middleton (Migsy), Bazza and Dave Hill, Mickey Wigley, 'our Dave', Bob Williams (Dandy Willow) – we've all cracked a pane or two in the street. Any window that caught it with the ball had to be paid for. After the initial cry of 'scarper!', accounts had to be settled. Each one of us would go home and sort out the pop bottles to take back. Tizer, Jusoda and the like gave you 3d a bottle; for the bigger Cheethams bottles you would get 6d. You would weigh them in and hand over the money for the glass to the unfortunate recipient of the wayward volley or badly timed hook shot. 'So sorry, Mrs. Jackson.'

The 1958 season was the start of my love affair with Walsall FC. The memory of 'Cannonball' Colin Taylor knocking down a Hartlepool player with one of his thunderbolts is as vivid today as it was back then. A stop off at the Bridge Café, Walsall for a hot dog lined with stuffing became a pre-match ritual. Great days beckoned for the Saddlers.

1958 saw my older brother Alan marry his childhood sweetheart and former Brownies 'snowdrop' troop veteran Jean Stokes. With Jean's mom being very ill at the time, the reception was held at No. 22, with mom feeding the masses in two sittings. The best man was Alan's army friend Pete Gillingham of Acton, London, who remains a family friend to this day. The celebrations carried on into the night, with the lucky adults legging it to The Crown, and the Anderson shelter again proved its worth when packed high with empties – the Blue Seal sherry bottles stayed there for years – empty, of course!

Most of the kids in our street attended Leamore Junior and Infants School. A fine school that bordered Leamore Park, football pitches and cricket strips, tennis courts, a putting green, bowling greens and beautiful flowerbeds and above all a 'Parkie'. The park is now a virtual wasteland – a sad sign of the times in which we now live.

In an age when the seasons actually seemed to be spring, summer, autumn and winter, the advent of the summer holidays was one of the highlights, along with Easter, Bonfire Night, Christmas and New Year, of course! The last week in July and the first week in August were the main holiday weeks. Our annual Beano took us not to Spain, but to Rhyl and a week in a caravan at Winkups Camp, Towyn.

We made the pilgrimage year in year out for at least ten years. Mom, dad, Granny Humphries, David and myself would get the train at Walsall station and head off for a week of sea, sand, sun and rain; with a bit of train spotting thrown in, these were good times to be a nipper. I invariably returned from Rhyl with a new football, or cricket bat, or both. Migsy and the boys would wait with bated breath – 'Is it a Wembley?' Wembley balls were the best plastic balls of all time, plenty of weight and a real joy to wellie!

After the annual Rhyl pilgrimage it was back to basics – dad at Harrison's pit in Great Wyrley and mom cleaning The Crown at Leamore – you were more or less on your own during the school holiday, apart from your friends, of course. Pebbles often rattled the bedroom window during summer, 'Come on, we're going over the Rockies!'. It was usually Dave Hill and Stunna. The Rockies, Clay

Colin Till on holiday in Rhyl.

Hills, Iron Bridge, Blue Lagoon, Ladies Head and the Mine Hole – these were all part of our industrial past and a great area to explore as a kid. 'The Rockies' was an industrial wasteland of heaped-up spoil, very light in colour, which backed into Hatherton Furnaces, off Leamore Lane. 'The Blue Lagoon' pool lay in this wasteland, pollution the key to its name. To reach the 'Rockies' you crossed the 'Iron Bridge' which once carried the railway over the cut to the furnaces. You crossed the bridge with trepidation as it had no decking and an early bath in the canal awaited the faint hearted! A short distance away lay the 'Clay Hills', the result of brick working and so on.

Follow the cut towards Leamore Lane and you came to the sunken barges, from which I was once saved from drowning after falling in. John Lowe was the hero that day. A hot bath and a clip round the ear were my rewards for that little escapade. Pass the barges and you come to the 'Lady's Head' Pool. Crossing Leamore Lane you come to the 'Mine Hole', or 'Marl Hole' as some people called it, an old clay pit with steep sides and large pool which was a delight to explore.

Following the railway line past Lambert's factory (now the car auctioneers) you crossed Green Lane into Beatrice Street where you found the 'Jungle' – just around the corner from Bagnall Street. The 'Jungle' was a small piece of ground with a few trees. There were more trees to be found a bit further afield, namely the 'First and Second Coppeys' (coppices). These were lovely woodlands to explore Short Heath way.

The above areas were strewn with small ponds and teeming with wildlife – newts, frogs, toads, butterflies, dragonflies, coots, moorhens, skylarks and fish. Fishing was a must; roach, perch, tench and gudgeon were all waiting to be caught. Working barges travelling up and down the canal were a regular sight in those not so far off days.

Characters were thick on the ground in those days – one such person being 'Oily Gough'. Oily lived near today's resident gypsy site on Willenhall Lane. After rounding up some of Oily's straying horses one day, we received an unexpected reward: a gallon of creosote! Dave Hill, Stunna and I had some explaining to do.

Corner shops were plentiful years ago. Jack Gallagher's at the top of the street and Miss Barge's on the corner of West Street were our favourite places. In Miss Barge's case it was because mom got 'tick' from there and also her cheese was spot on, cut with the wire, of course. Jack sold everything from Jubblies and Lucky Bags to Twist and fireworks. Twist was a chewing tobacco. Sold by the ounce it was a must for many a miner and dad was no exception.

We started collecting early for Bonfire Night, and taking the Guy round the houses was a ritual. One year we dressed up Dave Hill and wheeled him round in a barrow. We made a few bob as well! Fireworks were paid for with pocket money, pop bottle money and 'Penny-for the Guy' money. They were stored away as they were collected, ready for the big day. Ah, those roast spuds and chestnuts: why did they always have that burnt taste to them?

Number 22 Bagnall Street was open house to all and sundry: from the lads in the house crowding around our 'Ecko' television watching *Robin Hood*, to relatives such as Uncle Jack. Uncle Jack was a regular caller, usually after the pubs had closed. The rap on the front door, followed by a rendition of 'Nellie Dean' left you in no doubt as to who was on your doorstep. Always smartly dressed in a trench coat and white silk scarf, his visits were a joy to us kids, especially if he brought along one of his friends. One evening he was accompanied by a tramp, who nevertheless was invited in, fed, watered and stocked up with sandwiches and sent on his way. Sadly the old gent died in a fire some months later. On another occasion Uncle Jack was partnered by his friend, Frankie. 'I've had an argument with Hilda' said Jack. Aunt Hilda (Jack's wife) was a lovely woman, whom you didn't upset. 'Show them what she's done to us, Frankie!' Frankie opened his trench coat to reveal a shirt, ripped to shreds. Uncle Jack had somehow survived unscathed! Fuelled with tea and sandwiches the unlucky duo were soon on their way up Bagnall Street to my dad's cries of 'keep out of the hoss road!'

With Bonfire Night out of the way Christmas was on the horizon. A decent hair cut at Sally Sergeant's instead of your dad using your nut as target practice for his new 'hand clippers' signalled the approach of the big day. Christmas and the New Year brought the family together and we always had a good time.

Stories were told of yesteryear, and the war years, from 'Nank's' stint as an air-raid warden to mom's brush with the Luftwaffe! As mom made her way down the garden one day, a Heinkel bomber roared overhead just above the houses. Mom actually saw the pilot 'as clear as day' through the glass-fronted cockpit. Singing was part of family life in those days, especially so at Christmas. My Uncle Ben was only a small man but had the voice of a 'Lanza' and he always finished off a party – be it wedding, birthday or Christmas – with an emotional rendition of 'Bless This House'.

On that note I would also like to finish my story here. I hope you have enjoyed going back to those far-off days, those days of gas lamps and Lucky Bags.

Colin Till

The Beast of Bloxwich

It was mid August 1927, and I had been visiting my grandmother, Emily Bagley, at her house, No. 4 Moat Road, Pleck, Walsall. A staid, Victorian woman dressed all in black – a colour which totally belied her nature – as she was always a delight to visit, and one of the finest dancers I have ever seen. She was at that time head laundress at the union workhouse opposite (which is now part of the manor hospital) and she spent many hours regaling me with tales of the inmates. One of her duties was to bathe some of the poor souls that entered there and I recall her telling me of one woman who screamed the place down when stripped of her clothes, and who was covered from head to foot with lice, making her skin look alive.

We had spent that afternoon making flowers from crepe paper, tissue paper and wire, she could make any flower you can name. After she had made them, she would take a block of candle wax, melt it in a pan and dip the flowers in to coat them in wax, she would then tie them into bunches and sell them for 6d to neighbours and friends for pin money.

As the day wore on I was taken to the tram stop, to travel back to Bloxwich where I lived with Hubert and Anne Giles at No. 56 Clarendon Street, the sand bank. As I got off the tram at Bloxwich cenotaph, I was met and told that we must hurry home as there was a lion on the loose in Bloxwich!. We hastily made our way home, and the following day stories abounded in Bloxwich of the excitement of the previous evening.

Being mid August, Pat Collins' funfair had arrived for Bloxwich wake week. With them was a travelling circus, with lions, acrobats and other sideshows. They had set up on the wakes ground, at the rear of Pat Collins house and on the piece of land where the Asda supermarket now stands. Adjacent to this runs Church Street, which was at that time a row of terraced houses (some of which have now been demolished and replaced, but some are still standing). Apparently an old lady who lived in one of the houses in Church Street had been preparing a meal for her dog. S`he had called from the door several times for him,

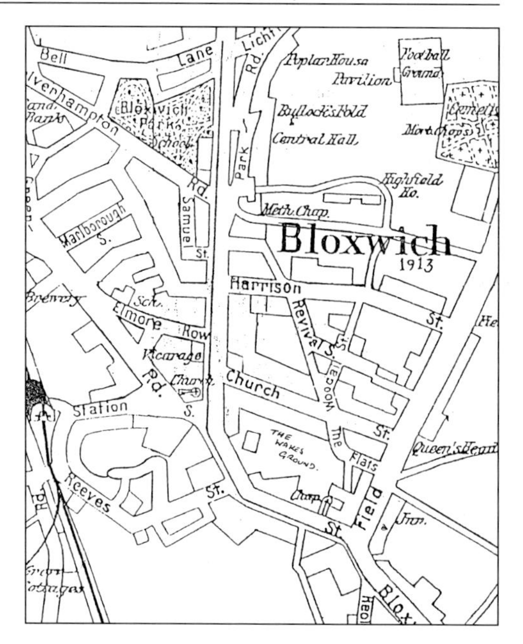

Bloxwich, the hunting ground of 'the Beast'.

but he had not come at her bidding. She had therefore decided to make herself a cup of tea before going to look for him. She filled the kettle and went to empty the teapot in the dustbin at the end of her yard. Just as she was depositing the old tea leaves she heard a mighty roar, and in a fit of panic upped skirts and ran into her neighbour's house, leaving the door to her own home open.

After explaining her fear to her neighbour, and the lion being nowhere in sight when viewed from the safety of a closed window, the authorities were informed. It ensued that the lion had run into the old lady's open house where it could be heard roaring, apparently at a view of itself in the mirror on the overmantle of the woman's living room. The lion tamer was fetched who came with a cage on wheels, complete with lioness to lure the lion back into the cage. It had apparently been let out in the first place by someone who had a grudge against one of the circus people.

This incident happened many, many years ago. I am now in my eighty-third year and live just around the corner from Church Street, in Revival Street, but I often think of the lion when I go that way.

Mary Giles

Memories of a boy in Aldridge

Memories of the past, local historical events and experiences have, over the years, been painted vividly on my mind to create a canvas of the rarest beauty, which I alone perceive, yet long have I felt the urge to share this wonderful work of art with others in the form of words and poetic verse.

My father, Edgar Wallace Birch, was born in Marsh Street, Walsall, in 1909. His father's brother, dad's uncle Wallace, was the proprietor of an electrical store in Stafford Street, 'Birch and Evans' which later became 'Birch Evans & Jellings' and moved to the Butts.

He was also an amateur thespian and a well-known member of the Grange players. My mother, maiden name Florrie Elsie Rudge was born and raised in a mid-terraced house on the Bloxwich Road in North Walsall. Her father, Frank Rudge, rented a smallholding overlooking the railway at North Walsall, where he sold eggs, goats milk and chickens to local residents.

Born in Bloxwich in November 1941, I consider myself a Walsall lad. Brought up by working class parents, educated at Aldridge Cooper Jordan Church School and later at Leighswood Secondary Modern, I left school with an average scholarship.

Aldridge to me has, and always will be, a fascinating village and must surely be the best place on earth. The very nature of the place has always thrilled me. Its country lanes and former ancient buildings, farms, duck ponds and relics of the past, though mostly gone are still clearly remembered.

In Grange Avenue where I lived as a boy,

open fields, pools and woodland lay undisturbed and free from pollution for many years. Wild animals in their natural habitat were abundant and a delight to see. Around these fields my friends and I could wander in safety gathering blackberries, mushrooms, picking crab apples, conkering or partaking in the occasional scrumping expedition.

We could wander over to the munitions dump in Castle Road, Walsall Wood, and pick up discarded bullet cases and anti-aircraft shells. They were all harmless of course. Or we could fish for newts, frogs, sticklebacks, and Jack Bannocks, which could easily be found in the boggy pools around Stinchcombe's Meadow, which lies adjacent to King Hayes Farm. At times we would wander over to the old iron-age fort on Castle Hill.

I travelled to school on the old Harper buses, and although their depot was in Heath Hayes near Cannock, every driver and conductor knew your parents, and if you misbehaved badly they didn't hesitate to inform them.

During winter the snow was sometimes so deep that it became impossible for the buses to continue their journey and we would have no bus service for two or three days.

The bus fare was a halfpenny from Walton Road to Aldridge in those days, and if the weather was dry I would run all the way to school so that I could spend my bus fare on sweets, locust beans, liquorice wood or sherbet suckers, which were readily available at the Jingle Shop, or broken biscuits from Aston's Bakery in the High Street.

In Coppice Road just a little way down the road from where I lived there were five small pools that lazily trickled one to another. All had fresh water supplied by a slow running brook. Each summer, local people used the larger one as a swimming bath, and if the

The Old Swan at Aldridge painted by Maurice Ivor Birch.

The Elms Hotel, Aidridge High Street, painted by Maurice Ivor Birch.

weather was hot, it would be swarming with young children, most of whom had their parents around to supervise them. The pools belonged to Jobern's Brick Works, or Aldridge Brick, Tile & Coal Company. They were uneconomical clay workings that had been abandoned. Tall chimneystacks and mountains of bricks cluttered the place, but each summer it was like being at Blackpool minus the illuminations.

Whilst still a pupil of Leighswood Senior School, two or three times each week I would go with my two best friends, Michael and John Smith, to their house. They were identical twins and lived in a tiny cottage almost at the end of Hobs Hole Lane, Aldridge, where it meets the Chester Road.

It was a beautiful little place. Their father, Harry Smith, had a huge garden where he grew almost every vegetable and fruit imaginable. Inside the cottage the old stew pot hung on a large hook over an open fire and the aroma made you drool. Outside, the rainwater ran directly into the water butt, which stood on the backyard, with the hand held posher beside it. Monday was the usual washday. They had no electricity or gas and were equipped with an outside toilet, which had to be pumped out periodically. Oil lamps were their only form of lighting except for a candle in the toilet where I spent many a happy half hour casting silhouettes on the rough white washed walls.

I would usually stay until dusk, then one twin or the other would walk with me half way up the lane, after this I would be on my own.

I remember that one particular night as I walked up the lane, alone and very frightened, as I encountered the first bend an owl flew from the trees screaming 'Woo! Woo! Woo!'. I moved like someone possessed until I got onto the main Walsall Wood Road, only to think how silly I had been, though thankfully relieved. Many a quiet evening the twins and

I would sit with the Romany gypsies by the side of their caravan, savouring hedgehog baked in clay, or enjoying a special drink made from herbs and wild berries, whilst their womenfolk sat making clothes pegs.

Sometimes the men would play guitars and fiddles and sing country folk songs with a sweetness of voice I will never forget.

A well-known gentleman resident of Aldridge in those days was a tramp called 'Cuckoo Bill'. He was a likeable chap, who stood about 4ft 8in tall, sported a big, white beard and carried a typical gentleman of the road's bag, attached to a stick and slung over his shoulder. When children called him names he would wave his stick at them in anger and threaten to report them to their headmaster, their parents or the police but, of course, he never did.

In the late 1950s and '60s many of the oldest buildings and dwellings in Aldridge were demolished, and Aldridge lost its former glory as if the Devil himself were on the rampage and destroyed them all. Its character has long since gone, but memories live on.

Aldridge used to be a sleepy little village where everyone knew each other. It was a quiet, undisturbed, antiquated retreat where bad things were unheard of and although it still is a lovely place, its character has changed completely.

I did numerous things over the years and met many famous people. From the tender age of ten I worked the West Midland club circuits, singing and entertaining to raise money for the poor, unfortunate children in Dr Barnardo's homes. In July 1956 I appeared on the Caroll Levis show at Dudley hippodrome. Today, I am a distinguished member of the International Society of Poetry and have had several poems and short stories published. I enjoy writing, drawing and general art. I believe life itself is wonderful and memories are too unique not to be shared with others.

Reminiscent of a boy, happiness things of
joy, air raid shelter, newters bog, red ash
drive, pea soup fog.
Brickyard pools, ferries wood, tall
chimneystacks, thick clay mud,
Stinchcombe's meadow, a weather vane,
black pit mounds, Hobs Hole Lane,
Fields of corn, the coppice pit, gas street
lamps, and... cuckoo spit.

Maurice Ivor Birch

Coalpool Pleasure Grounds

If you board a Bloxwich or Blakenall bus that goes via Coalpool and ask the driver for the 'Pleasure Grounds' he will probably look at you pityingly and then glance quickly around to see if there are any men in white coats chasing you. Then he may reply, 'Sorry, mate, wrong bus! Try the Blackpool one!' and escape at top speed.

Of course he would have good cause to doubt your sanity since the pool was filled in and all traces of the little playground obliterated roughly seventy years ago. Nevertheless, the bus stop at the bottom of Holden Crescent continued to be referred to as the Pleasure Grounds for many years after its demise. The pool was situated where what is now the junction of Ross Road and Coalpool Lane. A monument to this location exists in the form of No. 2 Coalpool Lane, built for the caretaker on the site of the Grounds in the early '30s.

My earliest recollections of Coalpool date back to the mid 1920s when I was a very young schoolboy, so things are a little hazy and should be regarded as no more than an impression.

I remember a very pleasant pool surrounded by trees, with an island in the middle, rather like a castle with a moat. There were swings and seesaws and amusements for the children to play on. The grown-ups could hire boats and row round the lake, or walk round, or sit at tables and enjoy refreshments from the stall, which sold ice cream, mineral water and cups of tea. To my young, eager, impressionable mind it was most enjoyable!

My next visit was really only passing through on the bus from Blakenall, after playing football for my old school team (St Patrick's) against St Peter's, on a beautifully kept pitch behind the King's Head inn at Blakenall, in March 1932. I remember the road was very narrow, just like a little country lane, bordered by Hawthorn hedgerows. I recall the sinking feeling in my stomach as we went over the little humpbacked canal bridge. This was before Coalpool Bridge was rebuilt, of course. I never dreamed that within six years I would be coming to Coalpool to live. By that time the pool had been filled in, the road widened and the rows of little old cottages were being demolished. The hawthorn hedgerows and garden allotments behind them, opposite the cemetery, had been replaced by new council houses and the remainder of the estate was nearing completion. The only job left to do was to slab the pavements.

The shops at Coalpool were already in existence although they have changed hands many times over the years. The Costcutters Store was built originally by the Walsall Co-operative Society as a grocery and house furnishing store during the late 1950s.

Returning in time to pre-war days the view from our front window was very pleasant. There were just green meadows and trees all the way to Rushall, with the little spire of St Mary's church poking up above the trees in the valley.

From the back of the house we looked out over green pastureland all the way to the houses in Webster Road. Beyond our back garden fence horses grazed peacefully, occasionally sauntering over to slake their thirst in a little pond in the corner of a field. This pond was later drained, as the gardens of nearby houses were prone to flooding during heavy rain.

In summing up, Coalpool was a pleasant little place in which to live in those days. It was almost rural – a little self-contained village with its own shops, a church, a chapel and a pub. This was no Shangri-La by any means, but I would like to end by quoting the well-known words of Richard Lewellyn as his character Huw, now an old man, is leaving the valley. He reaches the top of the pass, turns and looks back at the almost deserted village where he was born, the slag heaps forming a black scab over the once green mountains, the fields clothed with daffodils in the spring. Sadly he turns his back on his past happy life and memories of loved ones now departed, shakes his head sorrowfully and blinded by tears murmurs – 'Ah, how green was my valley then!'.

Ted Elwell

2 Walsall at Work

E.T. Holden & Son Ltd opened in 1819 on what is now the site of the Saddlers Centre. It closed in 1967 and moved to the site which currently houses Safeway but closed there in 1970 and moved once again, this time to Jedburgh, Scotland.

'Leather is my life'

It was perhaps inevitable that I would follow in the footsteps of my forbears and be employed in the leather industry in Walsall. Six generations and eight members of the family have worked in the trade; over 225 years doing various jobs all connected to the town's leather industry.

So, at the age of fourteen and leaving school, I was eventually taken on with two other boys where we were to be trained as apprentices at E.T. Holden & Son at No. 13 Park Street – where the Saddler's Centre now stands.

I picked up my first week's wages of 8s on 5 February 1940, included was the pay for Saturday, which we worked in those days. Over the following three and a half years we received training and instruction in all aspects of producing fine quality leathers for all types of items such as saddlery, harness, clothing, upholstery, patent leather and fancy leather for handbags, purses, wallets, briefcases.

The Second World War was upon us and in 1941 I joined the local ATC at Blue Coat School and eventually volunteered for the RAF in January 1943. I trained as a wireless operator and saw service in Norway, Holland and lastly Germany, until I was de-mobbed in October 1947 after four and a half years.

During this period I had met and married my wife, Muriel, and we had fifty-six years of

Ron Hawkins working with leather.

married life and two children together. Sadly she passed away in 2001.

After my return from the war I rejoined the firm to carry on with my training as a currier (leather dresser). I was eventually promoted to foreman due to the death of the owner of the factory, Mr Thomas Holden-White Snr, in 1955. His son, Thomas Holden-White Jr, took over and lots of alterations took place with the ensuing reorganization.

One amusing episode at the factory actually occurred on the day of the funeral of the boss. After the service at Great Barr we were all invited to the house by the boss's wife and were provided with lots of 'refreshment'. Later, fifty or so employees staggered up the driveway of the house completely sozzled, singing, shouting and altogether inebriated. The boss's wife smiled and said that her deceased husband would have loved it. He liked his drop of the hard stuff!

In 1950 I rejoined the ATC as a Warrant Officer instructor for the next generation of RAF boys, but had to resign in 1955 owing to pressure of work and more responsibilities.

In 1967 E.T. Holden closed in Park Street and moved to the empty factory of Handford Greatrex who were tanners and curriers in Walsall. This is the site on which Safeway stands today. At the same time I was promoted to assistant manager and it was then that I met the most exciting man in leather at that time, Mr Gorgio Gucci, the grandfather of the present Gucci family. He was in Walsall to order lots of leather for his businesses in various parts of Italy.

A lady at the Walsall Leather Museum once asked me why Italian leather is so much nicer than ours. My reply was how did she know that it was Italian? We were sending thousands of pounds of leather from Walsall to Italy to be made into goods which would find their way into places like Harrods at vastly inflated prices.

Eventually Holdens closed their factory in October 1970 to move to another tannery which they owned in Jedburgh in Scotland. I had the offer to move but declined and found employment at J. & E. Sedgwick on Reservoir Place on the Alumwell estate. They had previously been situated in Upper Rushall Street – now the site of the telephone exchange – and the firm is now over 100 years old. They were producing top class leather mainly for the horse trade and were supplying most of the saddlers in the town with their leather.

I stayed with them until my retirement from full time work in August 1990. I then joined the Leather Museum to do a job that I love very much: being a museum guide and demonstrator.

It was on 10 June 1988 that the museum was officially opened on the site of Wisemore, which formerly consisted of leather factories, built in 1891. Princess Anne came to do the honours and I was privileged to be able to talk to her and show her around the museum.

She asked me how long I had been in the trade in Walsall and I said 'forty-eight years' (at that time) and she remarked that I looked 'exceedingly well' on it.

In January 2001 I was very proud to receive the *Advertiser's* 'New Year's Honours' award for my sixtieth year in connection with the trade in Walsall and I am hoping for many more years yet.

It is strange to think that the leather trade in Walsall is actually descended from laces – yes the humble shoelace. By the late sixteenth century Walsall was primarily making metal objects, notably buckles which everyone needed in those days for their shoes. Eventually buckles were replaced by laces and as a result Walsall tradesmen tried to petition King George III to stop the spread of these 'new fangled' things. They failed, of course, and the 'lorimers' had to look elsewhere for

Skins for ladies evening wear.

Princess Anne visits the Leather Museum.

their trade. They turned to the making of bits, stirrups and all the metal parts of a horse's harness.

This eventually led to people taking advantage of the natural resources of the area, namely lime-oak, pork, beef and dairy cattle for their hides and skins, and to build tanneries for making leather, first for harnesses for heavy horses and then on to saddles and eventually light leather goods.

Of course war has in the past played a huge part in Walsall's prosperity, with the huge demands it created for leather for the cavalry and the various types of equipment for soldiers. Even today we still make a lot of saddles and equipment for the Horse Guards in London.

One of the strange things is that one of our Walsall saddlers is currently making side saddles for the American market. This is unbelievable in this day and age, but true.

One of the many jobs I am engaged in at the moment is working with the Trading Standards agency in Walsall where they can call me in for assistance when people have problems with their leather suits or clothing.

I have also been engaged in a minor role in consultancy work with businesses that have production problems and am sometimes able to help out by giving advice or making suggestions.

All this helps to keep me up to date with the many and varied changes in the production and manufacture of the thing I love most: leather.

Ron Hawkins

Memories of work

I started work at a shop called Hawkins of Preston in July 1961, which was half way up the street where the market was held. We did not have any tills, but the bills were written out by hand and placed with the money in a pod. This was then placed in a tube, which took it to the cash office where the bill was checked, and any change placed back in the pod and sent back to the assistant.

We worked from Monday to Saturday 9.00 a.m. to 6.00 p.m. with half day closing on Thursday. We had two fifteen-minute breaks and one hour for lunch. The shop was run on quite strict rules. The manager ruled the roost and everyone answered to him; his word was law. Next in line came the seniors who were in charge of each department and responsible for ordering the goods for their section and training the juniors. The juniors cleaned, tidied, made tea and did all the odd jobs as well as having to serve the customers. Everyone was addressed by surname, (Miss Jones or Mr Smith), and juniors never called any senior by their first name – even in break time this was classed as disrespectful. The uniforms were nylon overalls, first white, then later shorter and yellow, worn with a brown skirt.

I remember one morning hearing a bloodcurdling scream. We all rushed to the front of the shop and there running down Market Street was this figure dressed in black with a black cloak streaming out behind him. It was Screaming Lord Sutch, founder of the Monster Raving Loony Party who stood in many local elections.

In around August 1965 I moved to a shoe repair shop called Shoecraft opposite Woolworth's, taking in the shoes for repair and bagging them ready for collection. It was a very small shop, glass fronted with no staff room and a toilet out the back.

In our spare time we used to go to the Savoy or Imperial Cinemas. Sometimes on a Thursday afternoon we would go in at one and stay on until ten o'clock, seeing the main feature film twice. Our last bus home was 10.10 p.m. so we were never able to see the end of films or stay to the end of dances.

I went to the New Year's Eve dance at Walsall Town Hall when Erick Delaney and his band was top of the bill. Many years later in the '80s I went to a Welcome to Walsall festival and met him again. He was part of the entertainment and my daughter was in a dance troupe (OLCET) that had also been booked to entertain the crowds.

The Bridge used to have a statue of Sister Dora on it and some public toilets, which were underground. Every Christmas a policeman used to watch the crossing from some upstairs windows and if you crossed at the wrong time he would tell you off through a loud speaker after giving out your description.

One year a colleague was on the crossing when the elastic in her knickers broke and they fell round her ankles. Thinking no one had noticed she bent down, picked them up and put them in her pocket. Then a voice said 'I think the lady in the red coat and black boots should make sure she uses stronger elastic in her knickers.' Everyone turned around and looked at her as she fled back to the shop. It was a few days before she used the crossing again.

In the 1960s we used to go to Walsall Arboretum on Sundays during the summer to see what talent was on show. It was a great meeting place.

When I was in the Girl's Brigade in the late fifties, we all went to the arboretum to see the Queen. I cannot remember what the occasion was but we all had to line up to attention and salute as she drove past. Our company was the 1st Willenhall, based in Willenhall at Litchfield Baptist chapel.

We used to go dancing once a week in Walsall. I think it was called the Mayfield School of Dance. A couple used to give dancing lessons at the beginning of the evening and then there would be a break for soft drinks. We would finish off the evening dancing to pop records.

Trolley buses were a popular mode of public transport and would often keep running when the normal buses were stopped due to bad weather. The only drawback being that they could not run in a power cut or if the overhead lines broke.

I seem to remember we had more snow in the winters than we have now and some really bad foggy days. The buses were often prevented from running and we had a long walk home (about five miles) – no fun after a long day's work.

Mrs D.M. Guy

3 Religion

Yieldfields Hall.

St Thomas of Canterbury in Coalpool

During the eighteenth and early nineteenth centuries it was not easy to be a Roman Catholic in England. Churchgoing on Sundays was compulsory and the law of the land stated that everyone had to attend their local Church of England parish church. Those who refused were known as recusants. During the reign of Queen Elizabeth I both Catholic and Puritan recusants were fined. Those who offended constantly experienced more severe punishments such as imprisonment and a number suffered the ultimate penalty: death. Despite this, the old faith survived. This was mainly due to recusants using isolated buildings where it was easy to maintain secrecy. The seclusion of these properties also meant that it was possible to construct priests' holes in the night and to remove any telltale debris before daylight. One such place used by the Catholics of Walsall was Yieldfields Hall in North Bloxwich.

Even today it is easy to see why Yieldfields Hall was chosen. Situated on the old turnpike road to Stafford, the house was very isolated in the seventeenth century. Another major advantage was the superb view to the north and south from the attic windows. The Catholic family who lived at Yieldfields at this time risked persecution by allowing mass to be held there. In time however, a new political climate appeared in the country and two Catholic Relief Acts were passed in 1778 and 1791. This meant that Catholic worship and schools were recognized by law. In 1800 Father James Gordon left a sum of money for the endowment of a mission in the neighbourhood of Bloxwich. This money was used to purchase a house and workshop in Harden Lane (later to be known as Harden Road). The site of this house is now buried beneath Awlmakers Grove which leads to a new housing development. Incidentally, the nearby housing estate laid out in the 1920s has a number of names that reflect the pre Reformation history of Bloxwich.

The avenues near the cottage that housed St Thomas the Apostle were all named after former chantry lands which surrounded this area. During the fourteenth century it became popular to found chantries to celebrate masses for the souls of the founders. Chantry Avenue is named for the one founded in Bloxwich in 1515 for the Chapel of St Thomas, the Archbishop of Canterbury. This was a religious guild and had as its members both men and women. It had strong links with the town of Walsall and would meet in the Guildhall in Walsall High Street. The Guild was endowed with lands in Walsall and Bloxwich among other places until it was suppressed along with the chantries in 1547. In an attempt to put right some of the destruction wreaked under Henry VIII and Edward VI, Queen Mary allowed the former chantry lands to be used to found the grammar school named after her in Walsall.

After it was purchased, the house in Harden Lane was extended and converted into a chapel dedicated to St Thomas the Apostle. The first two priests were émigrés who came to England having fled the French Revolution. In 1807 Father Francis Martyn took over and enlarged the chapel to cope with the ever-growing number of converts in the district. According to Thomas Pearce in his *History and Directory of Walsall* (1813):

It is a small but neat place of worship, capable of containing between three or four hundred persons. It is adorned with some beautiful paintings – the altar-piece, representing the dead body of Our Saviour after its being taken down from the cross, is much admired.

The former chapel of St Thomas the Apostle.

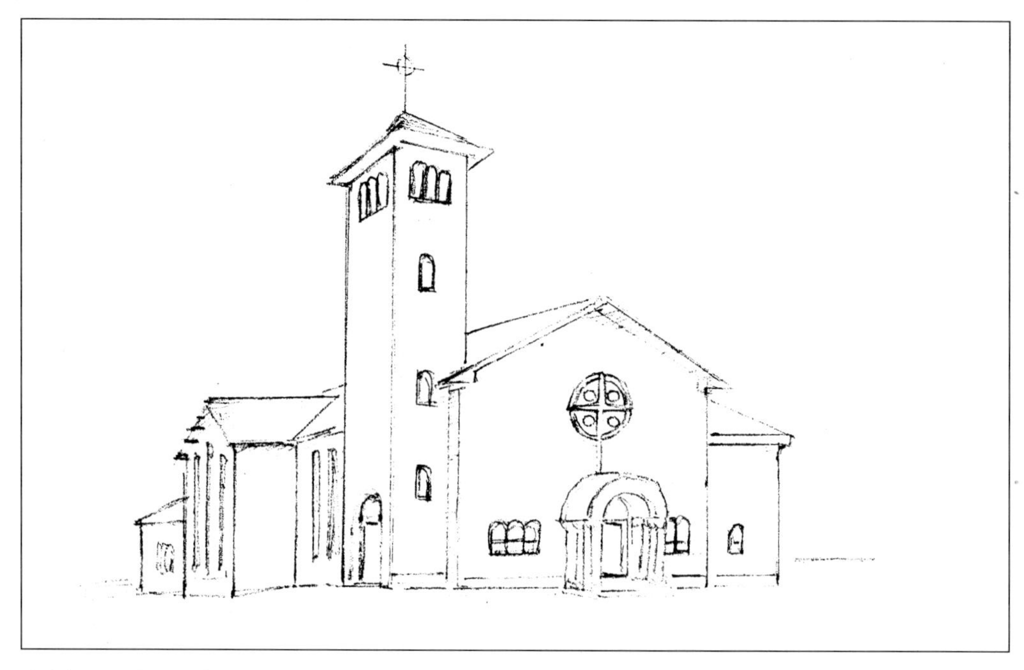

St Thomas of Canterbury.

From 1825 a Roman Catholic day school was held in a room next to the chapel. Father Martyn held a series of lectures about the Catholic faith which led to numerous conversions and in 1819 he established the chapel of St Mary in Walsall High Street. The site of this chapel is the Green Dragon public house, which survives to this day.

In 1869 St Thomas's was replaced by St Peter's in Bloxwich, but the shop survived and later became a ladies hairdressing business. It was, until recently demolished, the oldest building in the area. As he travelled towards Walsall, Father Martyn would have noticed the small hamlet about a mile to the east along Harden Lane known as Coalpool.

In the 1930s and the later 1940s a large number of council houses were built on former farmland in the Harden and Coalpool areas. The general increase in population meant an increase in the number of Catholics living in the area. In 1958 Father James Curtin was appointed priest to the newly formed parish for the Coalpool and Harden area. At first Father Curtin used Edgar Stammers school or Coalpool Library for Sunday mass. In 1959-60 the church of St Thomas of Canterbury was built on farmland in Dartmouth Avenue. St Thomas's was designed by Jennings, Homer & Lynch of Brierley Hill who had also designed the extension of St Peters in Bloxwich in 1952-54. The church of St Thomas of Canterbury is a substantial brick building, cruciform in shape with a south-west tower and an apsidal east end. Inside, the church the walls are adorned with fourteen stations of the cross which depict scenes from the Passion of Our Lord. There is also a very fine statue of St Thomas of Canterbury which has the Archbishops Mitre pierced with a sword to represent his martyrdom. During the last twelve months there has been a great improvement to the interior decoration of the church. A presbytery, completed in 1959, adjoins the church. Prior to this, the priest would have stayed at St Patrick's presbytery in

Blue Lane Walsall. The Roman Catholic population of St Thomas's parish in 1973 was 834 and has continued to grow. Perhaps the best way to describe the feelings of the parishioners for their new church is to read the words of the late Nora Long who was present during the first mass:

This Christmas, the parishioners of St Thomas of Canterbury Church are going to be to be cosy and warm, thanks to the new central heating. My thoughts go back to the cold Christmas night over 30 years ago, when the church was being built. Our dear Parish Priest, Father James Curtin RIP had set his heart on saying the very first Mass in the new church at Christmas, but when Christmas arrived, the church was just a shell, 4 walls and a roof, but no windows or doors, and an earth floor. But nothing daunted a band of volunteers who cleared away the builders rubble, and erected a makeshift altar, covered with a lovely altar-cloth. The pews were builders' planks, covered with lengths of wallpaper, propped up on bricks and boxes. I remember looking up through a hole in the wall and seeing the stars twinkling in the frosty night sky, and thinking that it must have been like this on that first Christmas night when Christ was born in the stable in Bethlehem.

Finally, an interesting link with the past occurs with the naming of nearby Whateley Avenue, Road and Place. These were named after Henry Whateley of Birchills Hall who in the eighteenth century handled the sale of Yiedfields Hall. The same Henry Whateley, in his will of August 1799 left annual payments of four guineas gained from income at Coalpool, to be distributed to the old and infirm people of Bloxwich. This was to be paid out on the feast day of St Thomas of Canterbury.

D. Miller.

4 Sporting Times

The captain and the secretary drove the first two balls – the grass was a source of trouble to various members.

Prize-winning entry

The secretary regrets... the club horse has died. A history of Walsall Golf Club, based on the club's official minute books.

The formative years

An inauguration meeting was held, at the insistence of Mr Howard Smith, of a limited number of gentlemen to consider the formation of a golf club. There attended Messrs. F.J. Cozens, J. Hemming, J. Myles, Revd J.W. Dixon and Mr Howard Smith

So states an entry in the club's official minute book on the 19 March 1907. At that meeting the decision was made to form a golf club subject to satisfactory negotiations between Lord Bradford from whom the land (at Gorway) would be leased. An interesting point is that, at the same time, Walsall cricket club was relocating their ground from Palfrey to Gorway and their transaction was also handled by Mr Howard Smith, a local solicitor. By 26 April an agreement had been signed by Lord Bradford to lease the land at an annual rent of 4 $\frac{1}{2}$% of the purchase price of £2,600 (£117 p.a.)

The following officers were elected:
Captain, Mr F.J. Cozens
Secretary, Mr Howard Smith
Treasurer, Mr H. Souttle

Committee: Revd J.W. Dixon, Mr A.N. Greatrix; Dr Sydenham; Mr J. Hemming; Mr R.H. Windle; Mr J. Mylis.

Most of these gentlemen were prominent figures in Walsall and the cricket club connection was strengthened by the fact that F.J. Cozens was now captain of both clubs. In fact he held the captaincy of Walsall Golf Club for four years, which was twice as long as most captains. During the last sixty years captains have been appointed for one year only and presidents for two years.

Following the meeting, a circular letter was drawn up inviting gentlemen to join for an entrance fee of four guineas and two guineas for non-Saturday members. Sunday play was not allowed and would not be until 1919. By May, 123 members had been accepted and subsequently two groundsmen were taken on. By this time the club had approached J.H. Oke – the professional at nearby Sutton Coldfield – to advise on the course layout and he staked out six holes. Like many golf professionals in his era he later sought fame in America.

The Walsall gentlemen were obviously in a hurry and in less than four months the course was opened. The minute book reports that on 19 August 1907 'the captain and secretary drove the first two balls – which chanced to be good ones – and the opening took place at 10.00 a.m. The course was rough in places and the grass was a source of trouble to various members, but on the whole, the meeting went off very well – the day being fine and warm.'

Tea was taken in the grounds of the 'Gables', a large three-storey house with a viewing balcony, situated on the bend of Gorway Road, which would have been directly opposite the entrance of the golf course. This fine gentlemen's residence belonged to the secretary, Mr Howard Smith, who leased it to the club for four years at a rent of £75 per annum. This agreement would appear from the minutes to have been a source of contention and was the subject of an extraordinary General Meeting in October 1908. The matter was resolved when a new clubhouse was built in 1911 at a cost of £450.

The secretary regrets... the club horse has died.

The new wooden building, designed by architects Thacker and Jeffries, boasted a general lounge, male and female dressing rooms, a bar, larder and kitchen, plus a bedroom for the steward. A verandah faced the course and a ladies tea-room faced Gorway Road. This clubhouse was demolished only a few years ago, having served Walsall Council for more than fifty years as an elaborate garden shed.

Mr Thomas Ball from Hoylake was engaged as a club professional at a wage not exceeding £1 per week. Since Mr Ball, Walsall Golf Club has enjoyed longevity of service with its professionals and to date has only had thirteen. Similarly, only seven Head Greenkeepers have been employed during the club's ninety-five-year history.

Within a year the course had been extended to fourteen holes. Finances, however, were strained and it was therefore decided to invite the formation of a ladies section with the aim

Sheep were allowed to roam the course.

of bringing in £100! After only twelve months, twenty-eight ladies joined; by November 1913, the ladies section had reached 100 members and the General Committee decided to take no more. To this day the ladies section remains at this level.

Ladies were allowed to play the course on Saturdays as long as they were off the first tee by 11.00 a.m. – current golfers will note that this is contrary to present practice and one assumes that most men would have worked on Saturday mornings and wanted the course clear thereafter.

A caddymaster was appointed who in turn organized first and second class caddies at a cost of 1d and 2d per round. He was also forbidden to buy alcoholic drinks and caddies were not allowed to smoke either on the course or in the hallway where they awaited their clients. Later they were prohibited from selling golf balls to members.

Sheep were allowed to roam to keep the grass under control. At various intervals their numbers were restricted to 500 and they were penned overnight. In 1912 a Mr Holmes was allowed to graze his goats at a cost of 10s 6d per annum. No tractors were available until 1938 when the club purchased a new one from Tildesly's of Walsall. Until then most of the work was done by the club horse. The minutes in December of 1908 note that the question of the club horse was left to the discretion of the Honourable Secretary and the vet who had been attending him. In the event of the necessity of slaughtering the club horse 'a replacement be bought at a cost not exceeding seven pounds'.

In May another horse was purchased from a Mr. Earnest Heath of Wednesbury at a cost of £35 – but not before a three-day trial costing 12s 6d per day had been successfully concluded. Annual costs for the horse in that year shown in the minute books amounted to £1 4s for shoeing and £7 5s for fodder. When the horse named Noble died many years later, the minute from January 1936 noted that 'The

The committee stood in sympathy.

secretary regrets to inform the committee that the club horse has died. The committee stood in sympathy'.

The First World War

The First World War proved to be a difficult period for the club as several members went off to fight and alas some never returned. Their names are inscribed on a memorial tablet located in the snooker room. Amongst them is the name of the club professional – Mr A. Higgins. A minute in 1914 states that the secretary was asked to remind Higgins that his duty lay with king and country. A couple of meetings later it was noted that he had enlisted. Naturally the committee agreed to keep his job open until he returned, but poor Higgins died early in 1918.

The course was reduced to nine holes for the duration of the war – part of it having been ploughed up to grow crops for the war effort. Post-war membership had recovered; by 1920 it stood at 273. The decision was taken to extend the course to eighteen holes and Dr Alistair MacKenzie, a prominent golf course designer, was approached and thus started an association with a man who went on to become the most famous of all golf architects.

Born of Scottish parents, Mackenzie designed such masterpieces as Augusta National, Cypress Point, Royal Melbourne and Lahinch. He never underestimated his own abilities and, at a time when similar professionals were charging around £10, he commanded a fee of £1000 plus expenses. Dr Mackenzie suggested altering two greens, laying nine new ones and scaling down fairways at a total cost of £2,000. Work was finished in early 1921.

Dr Alistair Mackenzie was approached.

The Ring Road course, number two

Within two years of the completion of this major work and its accompanying expense, the borough surveyor asked to meet the General Committee on 1 August 1923, when he outlined plans for a new ring road – The Broadway – which would unfortunately go straight through the golf course. The committee was not best pleased, having just spent a considerable sum on the course and, having finally got sixteen holes, stalling tactics were adopted. A sub-committee formed in August 1923 finally reached agreement with the corporation in March 1927. The Corporation would build a new golf course at its own expense and lease the land to the club on a twenty-one-year lease, with rent reviews every seven years. In addition £2,750 would be given to the club to build a new clubhouse. This was a good deal! The club re-hired Dr MacKenzie, now at the peak of his career.

The new course was located half a mile south of the original and in fact retained two holes: the current 10th and 12th. In January 1930 Dr MacKenzie was in America and the secretary was instructed to write to him 'reminding Dr MacKenzie that his duty lay with completing his task at Walsall and asking what on earth he was doing in America?'. He was of course finishing off his designs for Augusta National, which is now regarded as one of the finest courses in the world.

Walsall's new golf course was opened on 22 March 1930 and the STD scratch was assessed at 76. Today it is 71, no doubt reflecting the improvement in clubs, balls and the greater fitness of golfers. During the course of the next few years little of importance happened except a few humourous events, such as a member of Barclay's Bank being bitten by the

The pigeon problem.

steward's dog and complaints were made from the club about the stench from a nearby pigsty. Then came the pigeon incident.

It transpired that the son of the professional – Mr. Adwick – kept pigeons and they must have become a nuisance to members when putting on the final green. During Saturday morning pigeon races, flying from due south and coming in fairly low, they created mayhem as they flew over the eighteenth green whilst members were putting out. Following a heated debate, the minute of July 1935 stated 'the question of pigeons kept by the son of Adwick was brought forward and it was decided that they must not be allowed to fly.' Details of their fate are not known!

The Second World War

The Second World War had a considerable impact on the club. A blackout was in force and according to the minutes the ladies section was reminded to be 'more vigilant' (one shudders to think what they were up to). All competitions were cancelled. Trenches were laid across the course to prevent enemy aircraft landing and although most were filled in by the Royal Engineers in 1943, the ground was left furrowed at the 6th and 9th to provide extra hazards. In February 1941 a red light was installed to warn of air raids and in July of the same year damage was caused to the clubhouse by enemy action. Soon after, a steward of salvage was appointed. In July 1942 the club granted permission to the Home Guard to carry out gas demonstrations. Any active servicemen with golf handicaps billeted locally were allowed to play the course for free.

The ladies had to be reminded to be more vigilant.

In March 1945 the original course, renamed Gorway Golf Club, was ploughed up for farming and was never to be seen again.

It was at this time that the local authority approached the club and asked that part of the course be given over to grow wheat for the war effort. The committee delayed: advice was sought from the Greens Research Committee at Bingley, Yorkshire, who concluded that the land was not suitable for wheat but satisfactory for oats and barley. Agreement was reached in principle that half the course would be farmed.

The Committee procrastinated but by late 1944 it was obvious that the tide had turned for the Allies and subsequently the course was left alone.

Throughout the war, a hospital cup was played for, with all the proceeds going to the General Hospital. In 1944 a record sum of £359 7s 5d was raised (in excess of £10,000 today).

Post war

Following the war the club purchased the original honours board from the old Gorway course (now belonging to the Council) and also the war memorial tablet. Membership had fallen sharply and money-saving measures were instituted. In 1947 no less than twenty-two bunkers were filled in and sheep were allowed to graze the course in order to obtain extra income. This was discontinued at the end of 1942 and by the early '50s the club was sufficiently solvent to have installed an irrigation system for the greens and a general tree planting programme began and has continued until now.

During the 1960s the club's existence was seriously threatened when repeated attempts were made by various councillors to turn over all or parts of the course for housing (remember the land was leased by the Council to the club). These efforts were successfully repelled and in 1983 the club bought the land from the Council for £350,000.

In 2002 Walsall Golf Club is a thriving enterprise with more than 650 members. The clubhouse was completely refurbished in the late 1990s and the latest irrigation system has recently been installed. The course is fully developed, heavily bunkered and completely treelined, calling for golf of precision and accuracy.

Its future now seems secure.

Terry Henwood

Alfred Percy 'Tich' Freeman – Walsall Cricket Club professional 1937-38

In 1983 I purchased a book called *Tich Freeman and the Decline of the Leg Break Bowler* by David Lemmon. Prior to reading the book all I knew of Alfred Percy Freeman was that he stood 5ft 2ins tall (hence his nickname of 'Tich'); that he played for Kent between the two World Wars; that he took over 3,000 wickets in county cricket and that he played twelve tests for England.

In the last chapter, however, I learned a new piece of sporting trivia. The great bowler, a legend in his own lifetime, had trodden the turf of Gorway – home of my local cricket team, Walsall. On retiring from first class cricket in 1936, he played the next two seasons in the Birmingham and District League.

How had the amateur batsmen of Mitchells & Butlers and West Bromwich coped with the master of leg break and googly? I resolved to find out when time allowed. Well, early retirement afforded me the opportunity and I set about the task.

In four of the eight seasons immediately preceding 1933 Walsall had finished bottom of the Birmingham League. For three of the other four they were bottom but one. It was from this slough that the club rose to be champions (joint with West Bromwich Dartmouth) in 1933. A second place followed in 1934 before three successive championships.

The catalyst for this change in the club's fortunes was the appointment as captain of Maurice Kershaw Foster, the sixth son of the Reverend Henry Foster, the founder of the remarkable dynasty that dominated Worcestershire on their elevation to first class cricket. After making his debut for the county in 1908 he went on to make 157 appearances as an amateur, captaining the county from 1923 to 195. His inspired appointment as skipper of Walsall in 1933 was entirely the idea of the charismatic president of the club, Mr William 'Billy' Preston.

Preston had joined the club as a sixteen-year-old in February 1891 and after making a few good scores for the Second XI duly progressed to the first team. He later became captain and achieved one of the great ambitions of his life when Walsall claimed the League title in 1912. He realized another ambition in 1924 when he was elected MP for Walsall, but he was no politician, being a hard-headed businessman first and foremost. This career soon came to an end, as did that of many of his fellow Unionists in the 1929 elections. With this, he concentrated his non-business activities to his beloved cricket club, becoming President in 1931.

He then began the policy of recruiting top-class amateur players to his banner and soon a string of fine cricketers graced the First XI, so much so that rivals nicknamed the team 'Billy Preston's Circus'. Not that this bothered the club much as can be seen by the following couplet that appeared on the menu of one of the many championship dinners held in honour of another success:

> So long as we're champions why should it irk us
> That clubs less successful should dub us a circus?

To the base that the best amateurs provided, Preston added a professional topping – the first of which was Norman Backhouse. He was a

Blakenhall Heath Junior School, also known as 'The Sunshine School'. This is the first football team after the war, pictured in 1946. From left to right, back to front: Ivor Hackett, Eric Woolley, John Davis, John Butler, Gordon Hayward, Ken Grainger, Horace Law, Norman Till, Albert Hunt, Ron Povey, John Davis and John Butler. (Photograph provided by Norman Till).

Yorkshire spinner whose appearances for the county were limited due to the fact that Hedley Verity had made a place in the team his own. He, however, was a high-class performer, as his record ninety-five wickets for Walsall in the 1935 cricket season proved. He was tragically killed in a car crash at High Wycombe in November 1936.

Preston was negotiating with Test player (albeit only one Test) Harry Alexander when, for whatever reason, these talks broke down at just the time that Kent announced that the services of 'Tich' Freeman would not be required for the 1937 first-class season. The reason being that he was forty-eight years old and there was a desire to bring on a young spinner, Doug Wright. They marked his exceptional services with a grant of £250 and the continuance of his wages until the summer of 1937. Immediately Preston got in touch with the player and within days he accepted the club's offer of £12 10s per week for twenty weeks plus £100 benefit, guaranteed by the President.

Freeman's engagement as professional was greatly anticipated by the Walsall sporting public, the club even going to the expense of providing new three tier seating at a cost of £500. No doubt treasurers of the other nine league clubs prayed for a fine day when Walsall and their famous player came to call.

The first game, however, proved an anti-climax as Walsall suffered a defeat at the hands of Aston Unity, with Freeman being troubled by a wet ball and the lifelessness of the pitch. In fact his length was not of the almost mechanical precision it usually was and he sent down a number of full tosses. His three wickets cost eighty-one runs.

The two games over Whitsuntide against

Kidderminster and Smethwick did go some way to restore the optimism as he approached the form that was expected of him. The matches provided eleven wickets for ninety-one runs.

Gradually as the season progressed through the summer the pitches became faster and 'Tich' came more into his own. Six for sixty-six versus Stourbridge was quickly followed by the dismissal of nine of the Moseley side in less than ten overs for just twenty-one. The last six fell for just two singles in 3.4 overs, his flight and speed off the turf deceiving them. Dudley were skittled for just fifty-four with Freeman bagging a seven for twenty-three. Seven Old Hill wickets for sixty-six completed a half season tally of forty-seven wickets at an average of just ten and the talk was that Freeman was on for the famed 100 wickets in a Birmingham league season, the record being held by his predecessor as Walsall professional, Norman Backhouse, with ninety-five.

Walsall gained revenge for their opening game defeat by Aston Unity as Freeman started the second part of the season with seven for thirty-four, which included a hat-trick (in fact he took four wickets in five balls). The attendance for this match reached a staggering 2,500 souls; this was followed by an even more remarkable 3,500 for the visit of Old Hill.

The club was so pleased that they made the announcement before the game against Smethwick, that 'Tich' Freeman had been re-engaged as professional for the 1938 season. He responded by collecting eight wickets for just forty-one runs and a seven for twenty-eight versus Stourbridge.

So it was that with three games to go Freeman had accumulated eighty wickets. But his luck with the weather deserted him, for the marvellous weather of the league season broke down and the first of these three matches were abandoned without a ball being bowled. So he needed to take all the wickets available in the last two games to match the hundred – a tall order surely.

Well, the visit to Dudley proved a spectacular piece of bowling as the home side were reduced to ninety-four all out. 'Tich' opened the bowling and after sending down twenty-one overs he finished the match by taking his tenth wicket for just forty-four runs. In addition to performing a hat-trick, he twice took two wickets with consecutive balls and only a dropped catch denied him a second hat-trick.

So to the last match of the season, the visit of West Bromwich Dartmouth to Gorway. An occasion marked by the granting to each visitor to the ground a ticket for a free bottle of beer with which to toast the Club's Championship, which had been won weeks before in record time.

Shortly after 6 p.m. the last match of the season was over and the President delivered a speech from the steps of the pavilion exalting his team's success. Cheers rang out despite the fact that Walsall had lost the game and Freeman had only taken eight wickets for fifty-two runs. The snap had seemed to go out

Alfred Percy 'Tich' Freeman.

of the team despite restricting Dartmouth to ninety-four they themselves succumbed to sixty-four all out.

Billy Preston was amply rewarded for his enterprise in securing Freeman at the highest remuneration ever paid to a professional in the Birmingham League when 'Tich' set a new league record of ninety-eight wickets. Incidentally this record still stands today.

On receiving the ball, suitably mounted, with which he had taken all ten wickets against Dudley, 'Tich' stated that he had enjoyed this cricket more than any in which he had played and that he never realized the Birmingham League standard was so high or so keen.

Freeman's second season started well with four for forty-four against Smethwick in the opening game, followed by a poor two for sixty against his bogey side, Mitchells and Butlers. They were possibly the best team in the League at the time, despite not fulfilling their potential, and Freeman never dominated in any of his four games against them; his best figures being a three for fifty-eight (1938) and his worst one for eighty (1937).

However, it was with the bat that 'Tich' and subsequently Walsall were to suffer regrets at the season's end. Mitchells & Butlers had posted 178 runs and despite a disastrous start, Walsall, having lost their first three wickets for six runs, staged a comeback. When the sixth wicket went down they required just twenty to win, but the advantage melted away and two more runs were wanted with the last two men at the wicket. Freeman, enjoying his usual position as number eleven in the order, was one of them. Two singles made the scores level and, with fifteen minutes of play still available, if 'Tich' had been content to wait for the right ball, the game could have been won. Unfortunately, he could not resist the second ball he received and he danced down the wicket to hit a sky ball to mid-off. The match was tied affording only one and a half points instead of three.

The next game, against Stourbridge, turned again on the last wicket. This time it was Freeman's inability to dismiss the last batsman that cost them another win, with Stourbridge hanging on for the draw.

There was now a lapse in form as Freeman returned disappointing figures of three for fifty-four versus Moseley and one for forty-nine versus Kidderminster. The game against Aston Unity was lost despite his five for forty-four. In fact he never took more than five wickets in a match for Walsall again.

It was about this time that he did not open the bowling and in some cases was not the first change despite in one match taking four for twenty-eight in 6.3 overs. A further loss, this time to Moseley, when again Freeman's figures were disappointing (two for eighty-nine), caused a minor financial crisis as the lack of success was beginning to be reflected in declining gates.

Then came a morale boosting win against Mitchells & Butlers and with other contenders for the title Smethwick and Kidderminster faltering, the race was now down to two – Walsall and Moseley. This coincided with a return to form by 'Tich' as he had a five for thirty-seven versus Stourbridge and a five for ninety against Old Hill. The later game, however, was a draw and Moseley went into the last game with a lead of one and a half points and, as both teams won their remaining game, they were declared champions.

Whatever the reasons for Walsall's failure, the indifferent batting and poor fielding that was prevalent in both 1937 and 1938 were forgotten. It was the tied game against Mitchells & Butlers and Freeman's part in it that stayed in the memory. His haul of seventy-five wickets did not save him from criticism for his happy-go-lucky shot that cost Walsall the one and a half points needed for a joint share of the championship.

Whether this criticism was carried over to the annual meeting of the club in April 1939 and influenced the decision to dispense with a professional for the coming season is unclear. The president and the ex captain, Maurice Foster, who resigned at the end of 1937, expressed misgivings. However, the skipper, Norman Partridge, himself an outstanding amateur bowler, was much in favour, as were the majority of the committee members. The argument was that the amateur talent available to the club would more than compensate. It was also noted that Moseley had won the championship without a professional in their ranks.

Another area discussed was that the professional was supposed to provide coaching to the general membership of the club, a service Freeman never undertook. Mr Foster defended the senior player by stating that a man of his age and experience could not be expected to coach those who knew little about the subtleties of the game.

Perhaps the real reason for this decision is revealed in the financial statement presented by Mr K.N. Cooke, the honorary treasurer. In it he said that all but £6 of the first team gate receipts of £359 had been swallowed up by the salary and bonus paid to Freeman. Privately, after the meeting, he said that doing without a paid player would enable him to look the bank manager in the eye again. So it seems likely that the decision was purely an economic one. Of course, even if they had decided to have a professional for the 1939 season, it seems unlikely that Freeman would have been the club's choice. He was over 50 and the travelling to the West Midlands on Thursdays and the return to Kent on the Saturday evenings had proved a strain.

As a footnote, the 1939 season was a disappointment to the club. It was disastrous financially and unsatisfactory from a playing point of view in comparison with the preceding six years. Four wins and ten draws mean they finished sixth to Mitchells & Butlers in the championship. The slip down the table was attributed primarily to the ill-advised decision to try a season without professional assistance. This was rescinded when the season was a few weeks old but the field of selection was seriously limited. The president, Mr Preston, made approaches to another former England test player, Maurice Tate, who was still available. He duly arrived on the same fee as 'Tich'

Terry Harrison

5 Personal Memories

Granddad Bradley.

Memories of Walsall

My first memory of Walsall is of one June night in 1947. I was six years old. This was when my mother, in tears, woke me as she was carrying me from my bed into the waiting police car. It was the first time that I had ridden in a car, but I was too tired to notice where I was, and the motion soon rocked me back to sleep. I did not realize that my mother was so upset because her father (my granddad Bradley) had died, and because of that, life for me in Cannock was not to be.

I slept for the entire journey from Cannock to Walsall and so I have no memory of arriving at Hill Street. The only recollection I have of the few days that followed is the sadness that was all around me and the host of people that came to see my Granddad as he lay in his coffin in the front room.

After the funeral mother and father decided to move to Walsall permanently to be close to Nan, not that she was alone, as she had two other daughters, Florrie and Alice. To this day I look on Alice as the big sister I never had and we are still very close. The house was small with one living room and a kitchen while upstairs there were one and a half bedrooms.

This was so-called because one of the rooms was open to the staircase; it was more like a large landing.

There was no running water in the house, we got that from a tap in the yard. Outside the yard was where the toilets were. We had four toilets for the seven houses that were in the street. Also we had to keep the coal for the fires underneath the stairs. This was for heating and cooking as there was no electricity or gas in the houses, and lighting was by paraffin lamps or candles.

After some months one of the houses became empty and we managed to rent it. Mother got a job at the Grove Laundry and father still worked at the pit in Cannock.

I started going to Blue Coat Infants school, which at the time was in Bath Street, fortunately not too far from where I lived as I had to go out of the house at five to eight – the time mother left for work. This meant that I was always first in the playground and I hated it.

Alice and Wendy Hall.

No one had much money in the street, and us children made a lot of our own toys, like upside-down empty tin cans with string threaded to make loops that we could hold on to so we could walk on them like stilts. We also made dolls out of pipe cleaners, dolls houses out of cardboard boxes and lots more things.

William Bradley, 1947.

I remember my first Bonfire Night that year; it was something magical. For weeks the children of the houses in the small yard that was Hill Street went out, knocking on doors and asking for things for the bonfire. This collection of firewood was kept in one of the toilets that did not work and had no roof on, or indeed a door. To keep it safe we made one of the older children keep watch all night to guard it. This we should not have done, but being young we did not know that he was suffering from Tuberculosis and he wanted to help. (He died in his early twenties).

On bonfire night all the people from the

Mum and Dad outside the Wellington pub.

houses gathered and the men lit the few fireworks that we had between us. We all gave shouts of amazement at the colours and the spectacle of the rockets flying up into the black night sky, the spinning Catherine wheels and the bangs of the jumping jacks. Then the fire was lit. It was very high – so high in fact that it had not been burning for long before the police and the fire brigade came and told us to move it. It was dangerously close to the telephone wires of the leather-tanning factory that was next to the first house in the street. That for us children was an added adventure and we soon had the fire started elsewhere, with a few potatoes cooked in the fire to share. As the fire died down we all sat singing songs, the grown-ups even had a dance, then it was time for bed. As we had to carry all the water into the house, bath night was only on a Friday. I had a soapy flannel wiped over me and was sent to bed with a brick that had been warmed up in the oven and wrapped in a piece of old flannel to keep me warm. This was my hot water bottle.

Walsall was not just a town of industry but also a town with lots of things to keep the townsfolk amused. I joined the library and went at least twice a week but not only to change my books: in those days there were books on one side and stuffed birds and their eggs and other things on the other. I never knew there were that many different types of bird and I loved spending time there.

There were six or seven picture houses (cinemas) just in the town centre, from the 'flea pit', as we called one of them, to the posh ones like the Savoy and the Gaumont. If and when we could get sixpence, Alice and I would go to the Palace or the Empire pictures, as it was cheaper there, especially as sometimes we would sit on one of the steps instead of a seat and get in cheaper. There were always two films on, and if one was not suitable for children to see on their own, then we would stand outside and ask people to take us in. One day we were taken into the Palace cinema by a young man of about nineteen. He bought us an ice cream, a bag of popcorn and a drink, then he moved to a different part of the cinema. When we told our parents, they were not very pleased with us and stopped us going for a while.

The arboretum was another place that we used to spend a lot of time. In the school holidays we were there all day. We took a bottle of water into which we put a penny fizzer so that it tasted a bit like pop, and some jam sandwiches. We couldn't get back into the house until mom came home from work.

The winter of 1947 was very severe, but I don't remember it as I was ill with double

Meeting Father Christmas at the Co-op.

Florrie's wedding.

pneumonia and almost died. It seems I missed out on all the fun; local children had obtained a flat-bottomed boat which they were using to slide down Church Hill on the snow, until the police came and put a stop to it.

My Nan nursed me back to health. One night as she sat with me, a mouse ran across the floor and up the curtains. As I was lying on the settee underneath the window that the curtains were covering, my Nan, afraid that the mouse would fall onto me, grabbed it, squeezed it then threw it into the fire.

My first Christmas in Walsall was passed in illness, but the next passed in a flurry of activity, as we all helped to make the decorations for the house, and the 'tree' which was two hoops, one inside the other, then decorated with crepe paper of various colours.

On Christmas Eve a stocking would be hung up over the fireplace. The next morning there would be inside some nuts, an apple, a tangerine, and a small bar of Cadbury's chocolate, six squares with animal shapes on. We were lucky to get this as food was still rationed.

In 1948 we went to the seaside for the first time. It was to Rhyl and we stayed in a chalet, which had more space than the house in which we lived. It was still lit by paraffin lamps, and hanging on the bedstead was a bicycle lamp in case we had to go to the toilet in the night, but they were about 100 yards away, so we tried not to go until morning.

The next year my aunt Florrie got married, and Alice and myself were bridesmaids, showing off in our long dresses, then later that year they came on holiday with us. They had their own chalet close to ours, and they had a camera that they stood on a tripod – much better than our box brownie.

This next year I was eight, and one of my jobs was to go each Friday with Alice to change the accumulator for the wireless. This was also the year that I was deemed old enough to have a key so that I could light the fire for when mom came home from work, for her to cook the evening meal. I never quite got the hang of fire-lighting and ended up putting sugar and paraffin on to get it to light. Of course this made the sugar ration go quickly, but as mom and myself did not take sugar, dad never noticed. Before I lit the fire I had to light the paraffin lamp, this I didn't mind doing as I was afraid of the dark, but I didn't like having to trim the wick of the lamp, as I never did it properly.

I then filled the kettle from the tap in the yard and put it on the fire to boil. After making a pot of tea, the teapot was placed by the side of the fire to keep hot. The kettle was then refilled and returned to the fire to boil for dad to have a wash when he came home. As dad still worked as a miner, he was very black and dusty, so every night the zinc bath that hung on a nail outside the back door had to be brought in and enough water heated so that he could get clean.

The next special thing I remember was that in 1950 my Nan got married again at St Matthew's church. The party lasted for two whole days. It was not long after that we moved from Hill Street into a new house that had just been built in Primley Avenue. The houses in Hill Street had been condemned long before that but it seems we had been forgotten.

Nan with my dad on her wedding day.

Florence Roberts in 1920.

In January 1952, mom, dad and myself started to move the small things into the new house ourselves. We borrowed a pram and filled it, I carried a small suitcase, dad carried a large one, and we walked there and back, a couple of times. Then one Monday morning the council moving van came, loaded all our furniture – we hadn't got much – and took it to be fumigated to make sure that we were not taking any woodworm or such like into the new house.

Mom, myself and my aunt Florrie went ahead to await the arrival of the furniture, we

Wendy Hall and mom.

sat on orange boxes which were later used to light the fire. I loved the fact that the light came on at the touch of a switch; that hot water, as well as cold, came from a tap inside the house.

I was now a pupil at Blue Coat junior school, it was in Hanch place then, and quite a journey for me each day. I was also lucky enough to be in the netball team. I have happy memories of those days. The first few months were, to say the least, trying for mom, as dad insisted that the food should still be cooked on the fire. He said he could taste the gas from the gas cooker in his food. This of course was silly and in the end mom refused to do it.

We grew a lawn from grass seeds, both at the back and the front of the house. It was my job to cut them when they grew, the first time was with a pair of nail scissors, as they were the only ones we had.

Dad left the pit and got a job at Bentley Brick Yard which was quite close to the house. When the blackberries were out, dad and his work-mates would pick them at dinnertime, so that mom could make pies for them all to share. Although we had electricity, mom still washed with a dolly and a zinc tub filled with hot water, and a large mangle with two very large wooden rollers.

I remember in 1953 we had our first radiogram. It took pride of place in the room, but for over a month we had no records to play on it, then dad gave me ten shillings to buy one, and he wanted the change. As it happened it was in the school holidays and mom had given me money to go to the pictures with my friends. I dutifully got the record before going to the pictures so that I did not forget it. When the film ended I caught the bus home, but as I got up to get off at my stop, I forgot about the record and it fell and broke (in those days the records were delicate and easily broken). Dad was not very pleased as it had cost him 6s 9d and he had no record to play. After bouncing the broken pieces off my head, he sent me to bed. I was very careful with records from then on.

The next big happening in our household was when mom and myself talked dad into buying a television set. He was rather set in his ways and insisted that it would ruin our eyes, but just before I got married in 1958 he relented and bought one, and he became just as addicted to it as all of us.

As I still live in the same house, there are lots of things to remind me of my younger days and I smile to myself often as I remember growing up in Walsall.

Wendy Hodson

Walsall as seen by a visitor

I have never lived in Walsall but I do have memories of the town as it used to be. During the last war I lived at Perry Bar, North Birmingham. I would have been twelve or thirteen years old then and my father, who worked for Birmingham Co-op, would take the family to Walsall Market on a Wednesday, his half-day off. We would travel on the Midland Red bus from Perry Barr. This, of course, would be mainly during the school holidays and it was quite an adventure for me. My first memory of Walsall was the Sister Dora statue and my father, who was very keen on history, told me all about her. The old Market was a truly fascinating place for a young boy and I can well recall looking along the stalls up the old cobble-stoned hill surmounted by the church of St Matthews.

My mother did quite a lot of shopping at the market but the stall that caught my attention was selling day-old chicks. I think they were priced at 3d and 6d each. Most of these little creatures never survived more than twenty-four hours outside of an incubator but I persuaded father to buy me four. The trick was to keep them warm for the first few days, but we had no incubator. After we arrived home with them my mother had the bright idea of putting the cardboard box housing the

Bluecoat Junior School netball team.

St Matthew's church taken from Hill Street.

chicks on the gas stove plate rack over night, leaving one gas jet on very low and making sure, of course, that the gas meter was primed with a suitable coin. It worked like a charm and I raised all four chicks to full maturity. They were all cockerels, of course, so we never got any eggs out of that lot! Whenever I see young chicks I am always reminded of the old time at Walsall Market.

It was some years later that I renewed my acquaintance with Walsall. After serving with the Royal Navy I returned to civilian life and got a job servicing and installing radio and television sets. This was back in the early fifties and television had just taken off in a big way. I worked in the service department of a large furniture store combine, which had shops all over the country. The firm had a shop in Walsall, the Newday Furniture Stores in Park Street. I was a regular visitor to that store and I installed new television sets in many homes in Walsall housing estates and got to know the place very well indeed. Sometimes I would finish late and driving through Walsall in the dark I would see tongues of flame lighting up the far skyline. These were blast furnaces, of course, a sight that has now vanished forever!

I am now retired but I still regularly visit Walsall, now much changed, but when I walk through the market I am a little saddened that the old world vista that led the eye up to the church of St. Michael is now marred by some ugly buildings. I have heard that there are plans to restore this area and I look forward to that.

Ray Slater

South Walsall in the 1930s

My memories of the early 1930s are many: milk, bread and coal being delivered by horse and cart, all being regular timekeepers and having regular habits. This was the time before electric power and oil and gas providing the heat and light. Going to bed or the outside 'loo' at the end of the garden, we would use a lighted candle in an old jam jar for light. Going to the toilet in windy or bad weather was frightening, the flame flickered or would be blown out, so you would have to run back and have mom or dad relight it. To keep it going you could always use the newspaper hanging in the privy.

One of my early duties, when I was about five, was to walk from Chuckery to my gran's house in Emery Street, to pick up granddad's lunch in a basket. This consisted of cheese and onion sandwiches and a sterilized milk bottle (complete with spring-type stopper) full of strong tea. I then had to take it to the corner of Lysways street and Sandwell Street. I believe the company was called 'Frosts', where my granddad made stirrups from nickel. He was very good at his job. Only hand tools were used. I was once told that he made a pair of stirrups that opened automatically should the horse rider fall off, needed by the Royal stables for Queen Victoria.

In the 1938 war crisis we had a long holiday from school, and the late Dr Jenny Anderson's house at Six Ways was used by the army. Lorries and men were on the move all the time. On Sunday 3 September 1939, after finishing my delivery round of newspapers, I, along with other boys, was watching the activity of the soldiers, occasionally fetching cigarettes (Woodbines, 4d a packet) from the shop at the corner of Lysways Street when an idea came into my mind. I ran back to Grices paper shop in Ablewell Street. Mr Grice agreed to take me back with a heap of Sunday papers for sale. He must have been pleased as he paid me half a crown, 2s 6d, for the day. I normally received the same amount for delivering papers morning and evening. One round I covered the Butts area, Mellish Road and roads off, Broadway, Chuckery, Sutton Road and roads off, Daisy Bank then as far as the old Three Crowns public house, all on foot and then back home only to have to set off for school.

Mr L.G. Banks

6 Memories of the War Years

Celebrating VE Day.

Wartime memories

It was 1941; my husband Jack was stationed in the South of England, in the Army, with the Bomb Disposal Unit. I was working shifts with my mother, at Kynochs in Perry Barr making ammunition. Sometimes we had to walk the five miles back to Walsall with only torchlight to guide our way when bad weather forced the buses and trains to stop. However, one night a flat-backed lorry pulled up along the Walsall Road and offered a group of us a lift. We gratefully accepted and clambered aboard, not worrying about the dusty feeling when sitting down. On closer inspection, when we got off, we discovered the dust was black, we had been sitting on the back of a coal lorry!

In May of the previous year my husband-to-be was wounded in France and returned to England to recuperate. After hospitalization in Surrey he was given fourteen days leave. The first I knew of the leave was when he met me unexpectedly from work at Crabtrees Electrical in Lincoln Road and told me he had been able to take some sick leave from the Army. He had managed to obtain a special licence enabling us to be married in ten days

My wedding day, 6 September 1940.

time on Saturday 6 July. It was Thursday morning and I remember trying to explain weddings took planning at the best of times – we were entrenched in a war!

However, later that day we visited Father Sheeran, the parish priest at St Patrick's church in Blue Lane Walsall and the following day I went shopping in the town. I walked to the bridge to a shop called Mason Regent and in the window I saw a white wedding dress, and next to it was a pale pink bridesmaid dress. On enquiring I found that both dresses were the sizes I needed. We bought my wedding ring from Moss's Jewellers in Park Street and also ordered wedding flowers. I knew that trying to arrange any food and a wedding cake at such short notice during a war would be almost impossible. This is where I benefited from the tragedy of someone else. My mother visited Hindleys cake shop in Walsall and was told a local airman was shortly due to be married, but had been killed in action and the food and wedding cake were available. My mother kept this sad information to herself for a long time.

Saturday dawned, and we were duly married in bright sunshine, surrounded by family and friends. Unlike today's weddings, for photographs to be taken it was necessary for the wedding group to go to the photographer so we went to John Moore at the Horace Dudley Studio situated in Bradford Street. There were no colour photographs in those days.

The front room of my home held the buffet and in the middle of the table, in pride of place, stood the two-tier wedding cake, with fruit and cherries and thick white icing. Despite the constraints we had, it was a lovely day. The following Tuesday I remember us walking up Walsall market, where we bought a dinner service from a local trader called Benny Hood for the princely sum of one guinea! That night my husband returned to his posting and I was left thinking the previous few days had all been a dream.

Rationing became the norm and queuing for food a part of everyday life. We were most fortunate in having relatives in Canada who had emigrated before the war. I remember one particular evening arriving home from work tired and hungry, knowing it would be beans on toast again. A neighbour knocked on the door, having taken in a parcel for us. I'll always remember opening the lid and seeing tins of bacon, chicken and salmon, packets of tea, dried egg and fruit and also the luxury of nylon stockings instead of having to use sand and water, to colour our legs. We were truly blessed! During the war years many such parcels were delivered. Showing our thanks was difficult but we managed to repay them a little by knitting fairisle-patterned cardigans and jumpers. The wool could be bought in long skeins, wound into balls and joined together, or sometimes other garments were undone and the wool used again. Luckily, like our food parcels, they all reached their destination.

The arrival of the Anderson air-raid shelters in 1940 caused some excitement but the knowledge that they had to be erected by a certain period caused some concerns. However, if nothing else, the war bought out a 'togetherness' in friends and neighbours and everyone pitched in to help each other get the shelters safely erected and covered with earth by the deadline date of 11 June. There was no such deadline for their removal after the war, with many, like ours, remaining in the garden well into the 1950s.

The thoughts of the shelter always bring to mind one amusing story: on one particular night I recall hearing the sirens and making my way, with my mother, to the shelter in the garden. I did this quite quickly, as on a previous occasion I had failed to heed the warning of the siren and get out of bed, only to be blown out when a bomb exploded at Bates factory nearby in Hospital Street! I remember the vase of flowers on my windowsill was still intact, but the windowpane itself was cracked! On this occasion, together with my mother and her flask of tea, we settled down for the night, but sleeping was difficult, as it was a night of heavy raids. I lay there hearing the hum of yet more planes. After a while it fell silent and we relaxed knowing the air above was empty. A few moments later we heard footsteps of the path outside. My mother jumped up, 'It's a German, must have come out of a plane!' she cried. I can remember standing absolutely still for what seemed like hours and must have been seconds. Then came a tapping noise on the shelter. We looked at each other unsure of what to do next. Then my eyes landed on a small toy gun which my nephew had been playing with earlier in the day. I picked it up and moved towards the blanket covering the doorway. Pulling it to one side slightly I shouted 'Hands up, hands up!'. I saw a figure standing in front of me. A local accent replied 'Don't shoot, don't shoot!' It was our neighbour, a local Air Raid Warden. Sighing with relief I looked down at the gun and began to laugh. That 'gun' remained in the shelter for a long time. Well... you never knew who might drop in, did you?

Kath Taylor

The early 1950s. My daughter, with the air-raid shelter still in evidence.

Prisoners of War – learning to read around 1945

POW. POW... the strange letters hypnotized me as I waited in the queue at Mac's vegetable shop, trying hard not to be bored out of my infant mind. The letters were printed in big, white letters on the backs of the heavy, black jackets worn by a group of scruffy-looking dark haired men at the counter. Knobbly mountains of potatoes, cabbages and sprouts loomed on either side of the shop, and the smell of wet, soil-encrusted herden sacks, winter fog, tom-cat pee, bad breath, sweaty armpits and smelly feet was almost tangible.

On reflection it wasn't the first time I'd seen these men. They had marched along the bottom of our road in single file one day, holding spades and led by two men who shouted and seemed to carry big sticks. Walstead Road linked the Delves council estate with Bescot Junction. Again I recalled another scrap of memory. One blustering autumn day fat Aunt Violet, she of the carmine lipstick and barrack square bellow, had taken us on a walk to get from under mom's feet. 'We' were four, being 'like steps of stairs'. Big sister Margaret was quiet and wise, while at eight years old, Josy looked like a dour, blonde Shirley Temple. She was just one year older than my cross-eyed, straight-haired bespectacled self. Brother Keith occupied the old iron pushchair, lucky devil. Along past the sewerage farm we scurried, Violet leaning into the wind, which whistled eerily through the telegraph wires.

Rattling over the planked bridge that crossed the raging tributary of the River Teme, I tried not to look down through the cracks. At Delves Infants our teacher had told us the story of Billy Goat Gruff and I had nightmares about the troll, who I was convinced lived under this very bridge. The troll instilled such terror that I thought I would die of fright before reaching the sanctuary of the opposite bank. But then it had to be crossed coming back… on the day of the walk, just as we had done the reverse crossing, Violet shouted, 'Christ, Eye-ties' and started running hell-for-leather towards the safety of Shelley Road, the pushchair's wheels screaming in protest, we three sisters flying in her demented wake. Gaining the relative safety of Joseph Leckie School, sitting on the pavement to ease the stitch, I must have dared to ask Aunt Violet who the gypsy-looking men were. They must surely be somebody's daddies?

'Soft buggers, they got theirselfs captured.' I was none the wiser but daren't risk a clout round the ear with more questions. Margaret just looked away from my questioning glance, fearful of incurring bullying Violet's wrath.

Now, standing in Mac's queue, wedged between bus conductress Violet's fleshy thighs and mom's skinny hips, even my crossed, short-sighted eyes could see clearly the letters POW, the greasy, curly hair and darker complexion of these men who looked a bit like the gypsies that lived over at Delves Common. I had begged to be allowed to hold the ration books, but despite this fearful responsibility I was still consumed with curiosity about those puzzling letters. Overhead, the bacon slice whizzed to and fro, propelled by an unseen hand, the balance scales were fed with differing iron weights and robust paper bags were pummelled into shape by capable fists. Over and above this cacophony, robust Black Country housewives canted and cackled, their numerous urchin offspring bidden to unnatural silence. The worst crime was 'showing yerself up' and woe betide any child who dared to do so!

'POW!' Oh blow it. The intriguing word had escaped the careless censor of my infant tongue. A clout from mom knocked my steel rimmed glasses even more askew than usual. 'Shurrup our Joan. Stop showin' me up. Oi can't tearn round without yow actin' the goat. AN' stop wiping yer nose on yer sleeve. Our Margy don't do that. Dairty likkle sod.'

'No,' I thought rebelliously, 'not our saintly Sunday's Child Margaret. Only me wot was born on a Wednesday and was full of woe.' Twarn't fair. Anyroadup, our Keith wiped HIS nose on his sleeve and HE daint get half killed. Oh no.

I was too young to connect mom's dangerously low level of tolerance with her swollen belly, protruding like a cotton-covered football from her worn coat. Like POW, little in life made sense. Why, even just last week at the Welfare clinic, the doctor had put a plaster over my belly button, telling mom it might stop me wetting the bed. It hadn't, but a few days later Josy, in a moment of sibling rivalry or just plain jealousy, had simultaneously snatched off plaster AND glasses while I was (literally) minding my own business on the chamber pot. My eyes hadn't stopped watering for ages and I'd been terrified that I'd spring a leak from my belly button.

POW. POW. Everywhere I looked these letters shouted back at me – a word as strange as the funny language spoken by the Woodbine-smoking, famished-looking restless crowd of men now being served at the counter. Mrs Mac shouted at them as if they were dafties, speaking in an exaggeratedly slow voice and gesticulating wildly. Stealthily I caught Margaret's eye, my eyes large with unspoken questions, discreetly pointing to the back of the nearest POW wearing man. She bent her face to mine and whispered wistfully the classic phrase that has gone down in family lore: 'Theym foreign. I wish I'd been born foreign.'

No, she'd missed the point. It was the letter 'w' I was querying. It was almost as interesting looking as the letter 'x' in Oxo and oxydol, or the 'z' in Zebra Black lead, which mom used in polishing the grate. There was the beautiful letter 'q' on the Quaker Oats box, not to mention scrolled lettering on the numerous scabbed and rusty enamel signs outside shops, advertising Bisto, Coleman's Mustard or Reckits starch.

Silently I again touched Margaret's sleeve, then again indicated the problematic 'w'. A genteel finger to lips, a fearful glance at mom busily canting to Violet. 'The 'w' stands for 'war'' was all she whispered.

Well, whatever 'war' was, it had been going on for ages – ever since I could remember. Indeed, the trappings of war were as familiar to me as my own starfish hands. Blackout curtains, air-raid shelters, ration books and Mickey Mouse gas masks smelling of rubber and horribly claustrophobic. When I started school I had to wear the gas mask on a piece of string over my shoulder and it banged uncomfortably against bare legs. Opposite Marshall's grocery shop, on the corner of Walstead Road and Fulbrook Road, there was a huge open tank of filthy, litter-encrusted water, about three feet high, which we were told was to 'put out bombs'.

Looking up at this fascinating word POW I had a sudden flash of inspiration. P and O surely spelled 'po' and that was a rude word for a rude article. What had our po got to do with the war? Margaret took the coupons from me and began telling mum which ones she needed for today's purchases. It would be many years before we realized that our mother was severely dyslexic, but her eldest daughter simply took mum's difficulties in her capable stride, much as a child with a blind or deaf parent would do so. That was another thing long accepted, just like war. Looking back, perhaps that's why I got on mum's nerves – always asking questions about words.

Finally we were on our way home, the old pushchair screeching in protest as mom and Violet sped past the file of men now marching in crocodile formation towards Bescot and its ammunition producing factories. Holding on to the cold, metal pushchair, my arm was nearly wrenched out of its socket, my feet a blur pedalling mid-air.

Safely gaining the haven of our garden I made for my den hollowed out amongst the now rank weeds. Spirals of willow herb seeds curled in smoky question marks against the sky and dog-tired dog daisies drooped drearily. Much later I would hear the word 'melancholy' and finally put a word to the anguished feelings that threatened to overwhelm me on that particular day. It is only in retrospect that I realized I must have intuitively empathized with the Italian prisoners' sense of loss and longing, felt the lament of the dispossessed men so far from home.

Were my tears for them – or for myself? For something indefinable – a heart's longing – out of reach. Perhaps if I could make sense of POW, the other pieces of the puzzling jigsaw of life would fall into place. Josy, in passing, reminded me to stop picking the scabs off my knees. 'No wonder they'm always bleedin.' 'Ooh our Josy. That's a swear word. Our mom'll kill ya if er ears ya say bleedin'.

'Don't be puddled.' She brushed an errant curl from out of her forget-me-not blue eyes, regarding me with contempt. 'Am I puddled 'cos I can't read what it says on them mens' coats?'

'Ya know POW? I know W stands for war, but worrabout PO then? That's rude our Josy, ain't it?'

'They'm ITITIALS.' She spoke slowly as if I was indeed loopy. 'The P stands for Prisoner and the O stands for of… War. Prisoner of War, see?'

'Ow was I to know about initial wotsits, our Josy. I fort it was a propa weard.'

From then on, jackdaw-like, I gathered glittering piles of meaningless words such as 'crisis' and '*coup d'etat*', gleaned from newspaper headings and hoardings, syrup tins and washing powder boxes to add to POW. Then one bright day, sitting in Miss Farr's class at Delves Infants, pouring over the *Golden Realm Reader*, I suddenly realized I could read!

I suppose I was quite average really, being able to read at six years of age. Both Margy and Josy had, however, read at four, so I grew up in their combined shadow. But well before that day I had seen our next door neighbour's comic books and discovered there really was a word called POW – usually encapsulated in a balloon issuing from Desperate Dan's hairy fist. See, our Josy, I really could read at four – honest!

Jo Mary Stafford

This story was written after the publication of *Light in the Dust*, Jo Mary Stafford's biography (John Blake Publishing Ltd, London)

Yesterday, when I was young

I remember hot, sunny days; we had broken up from school. My friend, Doreen, called for me around 10.00 a.m. and we set off, complete with a bottle of water, some jam sandwiches and a clean hankie. The day stretched endlessly before us. All mom said was, 'Don't be late for your tea' – as if I ever was late for food!

Our first stop was a playground called 'Bulls Field' or to give it its proper name, Lea Meadow. Here we could swing to our heart's content, or go on the roundabout, staggering off dizzy, waiting for the world to stand still again. Then, on to the maypole, the shuffler or the helter-skelter. Woe betide you if you fell off – they were all set in concrete!

By now the sun was high in the heavens, so we would retire to a corner of the field to lie in the long grass, eating our bread and jam, making daisy chains if we were energetic enough. Rested and refreshed, we'd plan the next sortie, the railway, to watch the huge engines being turned on a turntable, or to sit on the electric box alongside the signal box. The big, iron monsters thundered past, belching out dense, black smoke and steam that made your eyes water and covered you with soot and grit. If the signalman spotted us, he would yell, 'get off that b***** box!', (fearing for our lives, no doubt). We flew over the Butts bridge, along Cecil Street, and onto the Fleam (pronounced flem). Here were the sixty steps. You could climb and watch the man below open and close the crossing gates to let trains and traffic go across, mainly horse and carts.

On to green fields with a wealth of buttercups, dog daisies' clover and lady smocks. We just had to pick a bunch for our moms. Then we'd have a paddle in the brook, our frocks tucked into our knickers (no modesty!) Tired and grubby we heard the hooter from the nearby factory and knew it was time to head for home. Would I get smacked for the grass stain on my frock? Maybe the flowers, now wilting rapidly, could be a peace offering to say, 'Sorry, mom'.

Home again, I was stood over while I washed the dirt away. 'Don't forget your neck!', mum yelled. 'Small chance!', I'd think. Then I had an egg with buttered soldiers for tea, a piece of bright yellow cake (which I hated but didn't dare refuse, otherwise I got a lecture on the starving children of Africa).

I was allowed to read until bedtime – that was after I'd washed the tea things up and set the table for when dad came home after work at about 7.30 p.m. I'd see dad for a brief kiss and cuddle, then it was a piggy back up the

Army days.

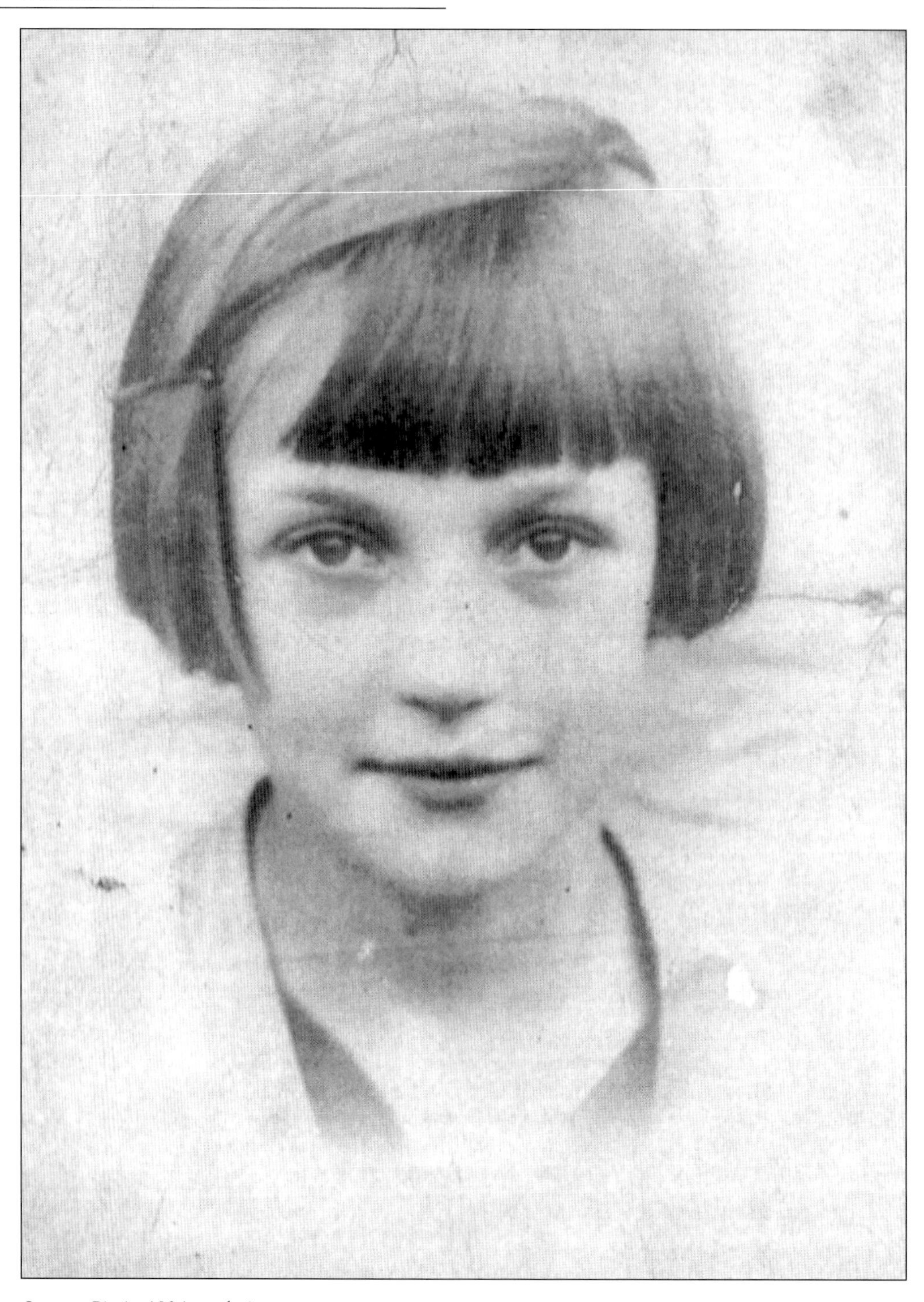

Leonora Pitt in 1934, aged nine.

'wooden hill to Bedfordshire'.

Sunday was special as dad was home all day. As a treat he would tie a cushion on the crossbar of his bike and take me over Bentley Common, now a big housing estate. He would show me the old coal mine workings of the Victory Pit where there stood an old pub of the same name. Dad would down a pint of mild beer, I had pop and a packet of Smith's crisps, searching for the twist of blue paper containing the salt, then home for dinner.

Sometimes I went with mom to take the Sunday joint to be roasted at Brooks, the baker's, in John Street. This entailed carrying it in a metal tin, covered with a pristine white tea towel emblazoned with 'Irish Linen' across it in red. We then proceeded to a smallholding in Brewer Street, where mom would buy potatoes and cabbage for dinner. On the way home, mom would call in the Lord Raglan for half a pint of bitter. No pop or crisps for me, mom wasn't as generous as dad! Mom stopped chatting and I hopped from leg to leg, worried in case I was late for Sunday School, but dinner was always on time. Doreen and I went to the Congregational chapel in North Street, but not before I'd washed the dinner crocks up, I may add. 'Not fair!', I used to think, 'My brother never does anything!' When I queried this I was told HE was a boy.

After Sunday School I'd wait eagerly for Jacko, the Italian ice cream man. He came round with a hand-pushed cart, water dripping from the ice packed around the tub, leaving a trail of water along the road. You always knew which direction he had taken. Mom would send me with a basin and tuppence. 'Don't forget to ask him for some wafers', she would shout after me. Then we had tinned peaches and ice cream for tea – luxury indeed!

Sundays were spent quietly, there were certain rules: no playing cards, chopping wood, or cutting with scissors. Mystified, I asked about this and was told 'the Devil will have his fingers on you!'. I still haven't worked that one out.

Children roamed far and wide in those days, unafraid, enjoying their freedom and their innocence. Parents, too, had more peace of mind. Yes, they were the good old days in some things but you can keep your black-leaded grates, your tin baths and your outside WC. Give me my shower, my telephone, my TV, but most of all my bus pass!

Leonora Pitt

A trip down Memory Lane

I stand in Ottakar's bookshop in Park Street, Walsall. I purchase a new book written jointly by Marguerite Patten and Jeannette Ewin, PhD. Marguerite was famous for her help and advice during the Second World War. She worked with the Ministry of Food, helping us to 'manage' our food rations and eat healthily.

I buy the book because the title is about beating arthritis and as my spouse and I are now in the big 'A' group, Arthritis and Aging – we think we will follow the advice therein.

I pay for the book and I am asked to help Ottakar's in a literature 'adventure' down memory lane.

I stand outside Park Street and my mind whirls back to pre-war times.

Park Street used to be a busy traffic thoroughfare – vehicles flowed up and down past the façade of the Victorian railway station and the Priory hotel. There was, I remember, an old fashioned chemist's shop – its large, brightly-coloured apothecary-style glass jars on the wall behind the counter, its deep oak drawers containing drugs, pills, potions, poisons? Who remembers?

Atkins grocers – very high class – had a bacon slicer on the counter; butter was sliced, patted, slapped, measured and weighed for customers' needs! Coin change was directed overhead by a pulley wiring system.

Another shop, a haberdashery, sold select items – hand-made gloves, corsetry, millinery, even feathers for ladies hats! My aunt (from London) came to Walsall especially to purchase these items!

The Red Lion is still with us – nowadays refurbished and repainted. The Savoy cinema has gone – Woolworth's is in its place. In 1942 we first saw the famous film *Gone with the Wind*, a four hour experience.

The Beaumont cinema, also gone now, brought us glamorous films to help us escape from the harsh reality of war. The Wurlitzer organ was a stunning sight, lit up, rising from the stage. The organ has lived in Devon for several years now. Local enthusiasts are negotiating to try to buy and bring it back to the Midlands.

The war years were hard, we worked long arduous hours, beset by bombing raids, but we enjoyed the cinemas and the local dances. Spouse and I met at a Pelsall Village Red Brass Dance in 1941.

He was in engineering, making tanks, and was also a member of air-raid protection (ARP). One night his village was hit by two bombs (near its Rail Marshalling Yards) and he was directed by the Officer-in-Charge to help measure the craters! The order was obeyed, the crater measured, he scrambled out – then one bomb immediately exploded! His duty done, he is still here to recount his story – luckily he was young and agile, and arthritis free!

In 1942 another air raid memory for me when I lived and worked in Wednesbury. Following one sleepless night I walked to my typist's job and had to pick my way carefully over mountains of rubble. Gas and water mains had burst, fire services were in attendance – a huge land mine had completely destroyed All Saints Church on the border of Wednesbury and Darlaston. However, the destruction of the Church had saved the nearby factories.

Later on, as America entered the war after Pearl Harbour, the GIs sauntered around Park Street, and the Town Hall witnessed their agility as their showed us their dance skills – the jitterbug!

Perhaps I have taken readers down memory Lane. Spouse and I have been married fifty-six years so memories are made of this.

I close by saying the years have brought comradeship, many friendships (pen friends, too) and close liaisons of all kinds – something to treasure!

Vera E. Astbury

Mr and Mrs Astbury, 18 May 1946.

Celebrations

Margo gazed with pleasure at the photographs of her grandchildren that her son, Colin, had just handed to her. They had been taken at the recent street party they had attended to celebrate the Queen's Golden Jubilee, and showed five-year-old Jack and two-year-old Elizabeth waving flags and smiling happily at the camera.

As she looked at the snaps, Margo found her mind going back more than half a century to another celebration and street party…

Little Margaret, as she had been called then, had been a very quiet, shy little girl and at the moment she was feeling rather anxious at the news she had just heard. There was going to be a street party and concert to celebrate the end of the war in Europe – VE Day it was called.

She was only six years old and did not properly understand what it meant. However, she was very pleased to learn that she would no longer be required to wear the gas mask that she had always hated, and screamed and fought so much when required to put it on. Also, the family would not have to move into the dark, damp Anderson shelter, which had been built at the bottom of the garden and fitted out with bunk beds – a wire lattice stretched across a wooden frame, with short flick out legs at the corners.

It had not been pleasant being roused from sleep and carried outside when air-raid warnings had sounded, the screaming siren, deafeningly loud. She had hated all the noise and feeling of fear that seemed to surround their trips down the dark garden. Night times were always very dark. Buses, bicycles, and the few private cars that were around all travelled without lights or beepers. The streets were only illumined with moonlight now, as the friendly man no longer came round at dusk to ignite the gas lamps that stood on the corners of the roads. No welcoming lights shone from the houses. They all had to have black-lined curtains, and even if a tiny chink of light showed from any house, the air raid warden (or ARPs as they came to be known) would bang on the door and demand that it be rectified immediately without hesitation. But that was all over now and everyone seemed to be relieved and happy.

The people who lived on Bescot Grange Estate had elected a committee to organize the celebration and they had asked that Margaret be allowed to appear as 'Miss England' at the concert that was to be staged in the Methodist Church Hall. Most of the other children were taking part, so she reluctantly agreed to attend.

When the day of the actual performance arrived, Little Margaret sat watching it in awe. Maisie Ackrill, who lived next door, wore a long white dress with a sash across the bodice with the word 'peace' sewn on to it. Lots of other people had sung and performed and her three friends walked on to the stage dressed as 'Miss Ireland', 'Miss Scotland' and 'Miss Wales'. Now it was the climax of the show, and it was her turn to walk from the wings to the centre of the stage. She was wearing a white dress that her mother had made from parachute silk, with a Union Jack on the front. She had a large bow made from red, white and blue ribbon in her blonde hair that had been curled under with the heating tongs especially in honour of the occasion. Her legs refused to move, but she was urged gently forward and greeted with tumultuous applause as the whole audience rose and everybody sang 'There'll Always Be An England'. It was a moment that she would remember for the rest of her life.

A street party followed with tables, chairs and benches laid out down the centre of the road. Pianos were dragged out onto the pavement and the merrymaking began! Food and drink had been obtained, although it was still rationed, and a good time was had by all. Her last memory of that day was the singing

Margaret Dickinson as Miss England in the post war pageant,

The Golden Jubilee.

in the street as she was carried sleepily indoors with her eyes stinging from the cigarette smoke.

As Margo dragged her mind back to the present day she remembered the key events that had taken place in her life between the two street parties. The birth of her brother Malcolm; her whirlwind marriage to Neville – a good, kind man who had given her Paul, now living in New Zealand, Clare, who inherited her mother's talent for music, and Colin, the father of Jack and Elizabeth.

Margo looked again at the photographs and felt an overwhelming sense of relief that there had indeed been peace in England for her grandchildren to enjoy.

Margo Trubshaw

7 Entertainment

Darlaston Rifle Corps Band, c. 1880. John Howl, centre, wearing a top hat.

The musical gene

My grandfather, John William Howl, was born in Darlaston in 1863, the fourth child and eldest son in a family passionate about music. It is sometimes assumed that in those days before radio and recording technology was invented, music was only heard in churches and chapels or on Saturday nights when music hall songs were belted out in the pubs. This was far from the truth. John's father, my great grandfather, born in 1832 and also named John, was similarly raised in a musical family. As a youth he was employed to blow the post horn on the stagecoach owned by his uncle Obadiah Howl, which carried travellers to Birmingham and back. The post horn was not the only instrument he could play. An original hand-written advertisement reads: 'John Howl gives lessons on the Piano Forte, Organ, Cornet-a-Pistons, Sax-Horn and Trumpet.' The sax-horn was an early tuba. In 1851 a group of musicians gave a benefit concert in the National School,

Willenhall on behalf of a young widow and her children. The concert comprised of a selection of music by Handel, Mozart and Haydn, and included 'Let The Bright Seraphim' from Sampson, sung by a certain Miss Phoebe Booth with trumpet obligato by Mr J. Howl. (This solo was sung by Dame Kiri Te Kanawa in St Paul's Cathedral on the occasion of the wedding of Prince Charles and Diana.) A copy of the concert programme has survived. Obviously it was a memento, for three years later John and Phoebe were married.

The early years of their married life were spent in a cottage in Cock Street, Darlaston, later renamed High Street as the residents demanded something more refined. My grandfather remembered as a boy climbing on the garden wall which backed on to the garden of Poplar House in King Street. In the summertime he often spotted Mrs Henry Wood, the romantic novelist and author of East Lynne, sitting in the shade of the arbour, writing. She was related to the family of Poplar House.

The census of 1881 records John Howl, father, 1a, The Bull Stake, as Professor of Music and owner of a music shop, selling instruments and sheet music. Around this time, he was organist at two churches, neither in Darlaston. This meant walking to and from Willenhall for morning service at St Giles', and then walking to and from Wednesbury for evening service at St Bartholomew's. Not exactly a day of rest, but in those days people were accustomed to walking. It was the only way of getting from one place to another for most people

Brass bands were very popular in the 1880s, with amateur musicians eager to join. John Howl was leader and conductor of the Darlaston Militia Rifle Corps Band. In 1887, Darlaston celebrated Queen Victoria's Jubilee with decorated streets and the foundation stone of the new town hall being laid. Four hundred needy people were supplied with dinner in a marquee erected in a field, and there was music from half past six to eight o'clock, when the Darlaston Rifle Corps Band, conducted by John Howl, were stationed in front of the Board Schools. The evening ended with a beacon fire and fireworks. In later years, John conducted the Havelock Band. Sadly, after attending some function, he returned home cold and tired, and sitting in a chair by the fire, suddenly collapsed and died. He was sixty-three.

The descriptions of his funeral filled the columns of the local newspapers. Referred to as 'this well known and highly respected musician', choirs from four churches sang at his memorial service and hundreds lined the streets as the Havelock Band led the funeral procession playing the Dead March from Saul. Phoebe continued singing at local concerts and according to her son 'She could sing high C as clear as a bird when seventy years of age.' The music shop was converted to a tobacconist's and it became a thriving concern, remaining in the family until the mid-1930s when my Aunt Winn left, and then continuing in other hands until the 1950s. As late as the 1960s a small tin-plate sign on the upper brickwork read John Howl.

My grandfather John Howl Jnr, who had received a good grounding in music from his father, gave lessons on the piano and organ while in his teens. He later went to Caernarvon College and became one of the first certificated teachers. His first teaching post was in Yeadon in Yorkshire, but before leaving Darlaston he married Betsy Annie Purcell. The ceremony took place at the old All Saint's church on the Walsall Road, later destroyed by German bombers in the Second World War. The newlyweds were driven to Walsall railway station in a pony and trap. Roads then were unpaved, stony and rutted, and passing the Globe Inn at Bescot Bridge, one of the wheels came off, and they were

Phoebe Booth in the doorway of the tobacconist's shop in Pinfold Street, Darlaston, c. 1900.

flung into the carriageway. Fortunately the proprietors of the inn came to the rescue and comforted the poor bride who was shaken but not hurt. Another conveyance was sent for, and the couple reached the station in time.

Although they were happy in the north, and made many friends there, the pull of the Midlands was very strong, as all their relatives were here. So when three years later John applied for, and was successful in obtaining, the Headship of Holy Trinity School in Short Heath, the family gladly moved south.

Once more they arrived at Walsall station, which at the time was situated in Station Street. A pony and trap had been sent from Short Heath to pick them up, but now there were two children in the family, a girl of two and a baby a few weeks old. They decided that my grandfather should go first, taking the luggage, then the driver would return for my grandmother and the children. After a long wait, she was relieved to be away at last, but it wasn't all plain sailing. As the driver turned into a crowded Park Street, they found themselves caught up in a parade complete with a band, clowns and elephants. Sanger's Circus was in town.

Short Heath was a small village in 1890. Holy Trinity School stood where the Parish Hall is today. From a small building with church-like windows in 1828, it grew in 1855 when a large oblong section with larger windows was added, together with a house for the schoolmaster at the far end. The school was typical of its era, a time when children were not taught in separate classrooms, but all together in one large schoolroom, the pupils grouped according to age around their teacher, while the Headmaster kept a close eye on proceedings sitting at his desk on a raised platform. Discipline was strict, it had to be, otherwise the task of teaching hundreds of

A group on the vicarage lawn.

children would have been impossible. The number of children on roll in 1900 was 319, but only 200 or so attended regularly. Things became easier when a new infant classroom was built out into the schoolyard around 1905. I remember the old school well, because my brother and I went to Sunday School there in the 1930s and '40s. The Reverend G. Holmes was vicar then.

When John Howl arrived in Short Heath he took on many responsibilities. Not only was he the 'Master' of the school, he was the Superintendent of the Sunday School (morning and afternoon sessions) and organist and Choirmaster at Holy Trinity church. He remained Superintendent for fourteen years, and organist and Choirmaster for twenty. Betsy Annie helped at church functions and taught sewing in the school when family life allowed. More children arrived, making six in all. Sadly, two died in infancy, their only son Jack and Marie the baby born in Yeadon. The surviving daughters were Constance, Winnifred, Doris and the youngest, Bessie, (born in January 1900, four days into the new century) who was my mother.

It was my Aunt Winn who remembered so much about life in the schoolhouse. Their sunny garden which overlooked the Vicarage garden and orchard, being able to see from her bedroom window the small field called 'Paradise' where the Sunday School treat, an afternoon of games and picnics, usually took place. She also remembered the concerts her father organized and took part in. The schoolroom was spacious enough to hold a stage, which was usually set up next to the party wall of the house. My mother remembers listening through the wall when she was considered too young to attend the concerts. During the winter months, 'conversaziones' were held. These were gatherings where speakers gave interesting talks, or sometimes there was music or singing, followed by refreshments. Then there would be dancing – waltzes, quadrilles, polkas, Sir Roger de Coverley and the Lancers. Granddad sang or played the piano, while Grandma loved to dance. Constance, the eldest daughter, also sang and later on my mother Bessie played the piano.

Bessie was to carry on the musical tradition. Taught by her father from an early age, she later became a pupil of Edward Dunton, ARCM, then living in Willenhall, and went on to be an Associate of the Royal College of Music herself. Mr Dunton was conductor and Musical Director of Willenhall and District Choral Society, and also of St Matthew's Institute Amateur Operatic Society in Walsall, and from around 1916 the piano accompanist for both societies was Miss Bessie Howe. I don't know when or why the family name changed from Howl to Howe, it may have been because my Grandfather wrote his name with a small l, easily mistaken for an 'e'. At any

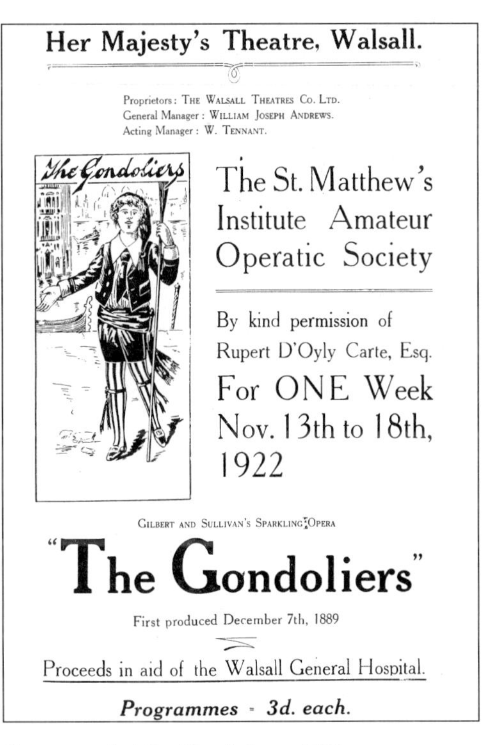

Programme for The Gondoliers, *1922.*

Percy Marshall in Iolanthe, *1921.*

Elsie Maynard in The Yeoman of the Guard *in 1923.*

rate, he was Mr Howe from then on, and later Councillor J.W. Howe serving first on the Parish Council, and then on Willenhall Urban District Council. Howe Crescent, off Lucknow Road was named after him.

St Matthew's Operatic Society were renowned for their productions of Gilbert and Sullivan operas which took place at the old Temperance Hall in Freer Street, or at Her Majesty's Theatre at the top of Park Street, the best theatre that Walsall ever had. The *Walsall Observer* critic reviewing *Iolanthe* in 1921 wrote Mr. Dunton conducted as a man who knew and loved his work much praise is due to him, and special reference should be made to the pianist, who rendered yeoman service.

In 1926, Bessie married Norman Matthews. My father was born in New Invention. He played the harmonium, piano and organ, being the organist at the Primitive Methodist church from boyhood. In 1917, he was conscripted into the Army but fortunately the war ended before he could be sent to France. After leaving the Army, he trained as a teacher at Chester College, and afterwards taught at Albion Road Junior School, Willenhall.

Norman and Bessie had three children, myself and my brothers Trevor and Philip. We were truly born to the sound of music as our mother gave music lessons! As a small child I was lulled to sleep, but I also remember evenings when I couldn't drop off as pupil after pupil knocked at the door then played their pieces and scales. In the 1930s and '40s the piano was so popular that my mother was

Edmund Spargo in The Gondoliers *in 1922.*

Norman Matthews, Flying Officer, 240 Willenhall and Darlaston Squadron.

obliged to give lessons all day on Saturdays.

My father had other musical ambitions. He composed music, not just for piano, but also orchestral works. In the mid-1930s he founded and conducted his own orchestra, recruiting every capable musician he could find in New Invention, Willenhall and Bloxwich. From a nucleus of five, the Orpheus Light Orchestra expanded to a band of seventeen players, describing themselves to the *Walsall Observer* as 'just ordinary working chaps'. The orchestra played light classical music and selections from musical comedies. I remember my father writing out pages of sheet music by hand and gilding music stands. In 1939 the *Walsall Observer* commented, 'Mr Matthews is a helpfully straightforward conductor – he is also a very able musician. His leadership is sound, and to that he adds the ability, invaluable in the circumstances, of being a capable arranger.'

All this was brought to an end when war was declared a few months later, as most of the instrumentalists joined the forces. My father, being too old at forty for active service, became a Flying Officer (Volunteer Reserve) with the 240 Squadron of the Air Training Corps, later the Darlaston and Willenhall Squadron. He trained the ATC Band to a high standard, and at the end of the war, he and the band marched in the Victory Parade past Walsall Town Hall.

Throughout the war, my father continued composing, and in the mid-1940s the Albion Orchestral Society played one of his compositions in a concert at Willenhall Baths Assembly Hall. The reviews were so good that he submitted some of his work to the BBC, and in 1947 Scintillation Waltz played by the Midland Light Orchestra, under Gilbert Vintner, was broadcast.

The family moved to Walsall in 1952 when Norman Matthews became senior Geography teacher at Blue Coat School. Here he set to music words written by Mary Keep (also a teacher at the school), which became the Blue Coat School Hymn. He retired from teaching in 1961, but continued composing and playing the organ. After serving as organist and choirmaster at St Anne's church, Willenhall, he was later organist at the rebuilt All Saint's in Darlaston.

The mid-1950s saw the inauguration of Walsall and District Operatic Society under the Musical Directorship of Wilfred Ellis. My mother, Bessie was offered and happily accepted the position of piano accompanist. In 1968, she was made a Life Member.

Looking back I think my parents were disappointed that their children were not interested in making music, although we played the piano. Occasionally my brothers,

Doris Stanley in Iolanthe *in 1921.*

A GRAND

CONCERT

will be given by

The Willenhall & District Choral Society

on

SUNDAY, DECEMBER 17TH, 1922

in the

Picture House, Stafford Street, Willenhall

ARTISTES—

Elocutionist - Miss KATRINA LUND

Solo Cello - LEONARD G. DENNIS

Accompanist - Miss BESSIE HOWE, A.R.C.M.

Conductor - EDWARD DUNTON, A.R.C.M.

Doors open at 7-30. Commence at 8 o'clock.

Programmes 2d. each.

Concert programme of the Willenhall Choral Society from 1922.

Walsall and District Operatic Society Dinner, 1966. Back row centre, Wilfred Ellis; centre of middle row, Norman and Bessie Matthews (by the flowers).

The Zenith Hot Stompers, c. 1982. trumpet, Chez Chesterman; trombone, Alan Bradley; clarinet, Roy Hubbard; banjo and guitar, Brian Melior; tuba and electric bass guitar, Phil Matthews.

Trevor and Phil, would try out a few notes on great-granddad's cornet – not easy listening! But they bought a *How to Play* tutor and improved. Then Phil purchased a trombone so that they could play together.

Around this time, Walsall jazzman Jim Shelley was looking for a tuba player and hearing that Phil played the cornet, asked if he would switch to the tuba, pointing out 'If you can play a cornet, you can play a tuba.' Confidence boosted, Phil obliged. It was the start of his career as a jazz musician. He formed his own band, The Tame River Jazz Band, then in 1966, joined Tommy Burton's Sportinghouse Four, making regular television appearances on *Pebble Mill at One*.

In 1973, he joined the Zenith Hot Stompers, appearing on television and radio and playing at many jazz festivals both here and abroad, also recording sixteen albums, including one with Humphrey Littleton and another with Chris Barber.

What would our great-grandfather Howl make of all this?

Lorna Phillips

Walsall dancing

My first dance as I recall was when a colleague from work took me along with him to St John's Church Hall in Pleck Road, Walsall. It was in 1955 and I was sixteen years old. We both worked at an iron foundry in Upper Brook Street off Queen Street and a number of girls from work were also at the dance. They seemed to want to make sure I had danced or at least tried to dance most of that evening. I found out months later that my friend had asked them to do this and it was nothing to do with my charm. Still, it boosted my ego at the time.

Other dance halls were visited, such as the Classic, an old picture house in Stafford Street. Although I only went in the evenings they also had lunch time sessions. Then there was the Regent, a church hall in Blakenall Lane. This was a favourite dance hall for me as it was within easy walking distance from where I lived on the Beechdale Estate.

The dance halls already mentioned did mostly Rock and Roll so for proper dancing, as we called it, the place to go was the Mayfair Ballroom in Bridge Street. This dance was run by Mr and Mrs Carrington. There was also a couple who taught ballroom dancing, but I can't remember their names. And there was George and Nell who were my aunt and uncle. George was on the door and Nell did cloakroom and refreshments. Mrs Carrington was quite strict and if she thought you had been drinking you were not allowed in. She also roamed the dance floor on occasions and you would receive a little tap on the head from her little cane and be told to stop if she thought you were not dancing correctly. If anyone misbehaved they were also told that they could not attend the next week.

Another dance was at the Town Hall. They had live bands such as Carl Wynn and Ronnie Hancox, whose singer was Susan Maughan. The dances tended to be a mixture of ballroom and Rock and Roll. The usual practice was to go early and get a pass out. This was a rubber stamp on the back of your hand which you had to make sure did not get rubbed off. Then it was off to the pub for a drink or two. There were many, many town centre pubs in those days and we all had our favourites. My friends and I used to visit the gentlemen only bar at the George Hotel. The barmaid was reputed to have been an ex-Bluebell girl, and she never denied it to us. Then we would go back to the upstairs lounge bar of the then Stork Hotel, a pub that has had many name changes over the years.

Another town centre dance was Redgates Ballroom in the Old Arcade. I cannot say much about this dance hall as I recall only attending once. I also went to a dance or two at the old Co-op hall in High Street, Bloxwich. And of course there were the dances at Bloxwich Baths when the pool was boarded over for part of the winter. An occasional Saturday night was spent at the dance in the Richards factory canteen at Darlaston, when a happy crowd of youngsters used to catch the last bus back home to the Beechdale.

John Mountford

The Savoy Cinema, Walsall

'Straight up the steps, first landing on the right'

These were not steps. These were the stairways to the stars! It was the staircase up which Rhett Butler carried Scarlett in *Gone with the Wind*, the staircase which Hedy Lamarr descended in *The Ziegfield Girls* and James Cagney danced down in *Yankee Doodle Dandy.*

Opulence was the word and the world of the Savoy Cinema in Walsall in around 1947. I was ten years old and clutching 4s in my hand and a note from my mum.

'Please let my son have two 1s 3d tickets for the show on Thursday May the 4th, near a toilet and as near the front as possible!'

The precious tickets clutched in my hand, I raced back down the stairs.

'Son, you forgot your change!' the man shouted after me. Change out of 4s to see the biggest comedy film star in the country (or in the world) as far as this ten-year-old was concerned. George Formby, in person, for one night only!

A year later at the Central Hall, Ablewell Street in Walsall I saw Isobel Bailey, renowned soprano, in Handel's *Messiah* and later, another diva, Joan Hammond, world famous soprano at the same venue.

Walsall then was a 'cultured' working-class town that housed six cinemas and two theatres. My father recalled seeing Gracie Fields, another huge singing star of stage and screen in *Mr Tower of London* at Her Majesty's Theatre in Park Street prior to its West End run. If it scored in Walsall, success elsewhere was assured. We could not forget the foresight of the young manager at the Gaumont Cinema in Bridge Street (in my day called the New Picture House), who every month, for one night only, screened one film which had been requested by his patrons. We saw *Henry V*, *Richard III*, *Hamlet*, *The Mikado* (and many others), all played to full houses until one tragic night when the cinema was burned down and eventually replaced by a Tesco supermarket.
That's entertainment?

Tom Rowley

8 The Best Years of our Lives

The North Walsall school strike of 1911

The scene is a warm summer day in 1911 in Derby Street, North Walsall. The children of the Junior School were returning gradually from their lunchtime break, no doubt thinking about how much more playing time could be got in before their concentration on various lessons. In those days the Headmaster, Mr Sammy Taylor, had a very disciplined staff, who all made sure the pupils gave of their best.

However, on this day an unusual occurrence was to take place that has not been repeated to this day. The early arrivals to school coming up and down Bloxwich Road and down Kent Street noticed something unusual in the shape of some fifty or more railwaymen standing about in the vicinity of North Walsall Railway Bridge.

As each tramcar rattled by from Walsall and Bloxwich more railwaymen alighted to add to the congregation. At the same time the children began to arrive in large numbers. With the crowd of railwaymen on the bridge and schoolchildren watching them in Derby Street, the playground was deserted for once! As time passed by, curiosity got the better of the North Walsall Junior School lads, who enquired about this strange gathering. Back came the reply from the railwaymen, 'Don't worry lads, we're on strike'. The railwaymen mixed among the schoolchildren to explain matters. It transpired that the Midland Railway signalman in the north Walsall Signal Box and the Porter-cum-ticket collector on North Walsall station did not want to come out on strike. The idea of the strikers was to turn out in numbers with a view to persuading the signalman and the porter to come out in sympathy. This had its effect and subsequently they joined the strikers.

The children were also affected by this spirit and decided amongst themselves to play a joke on their teachers. Just opposite the infants and junior schools running along Derby Street was a long wooden fence backed by a hawthorn hedge in front of the railwaymens' allotments. The whole of the junior school pupils – some sixty or seventy – decided to sit on this fence, side by side.

Meanwhile, in school, with five minutes to lessons, the duty yard teacher strolled into the playground to blow the whistle for assembly. To his utter amazement the playground was empty. Not ever having had this predicament before he gathered his wits and proceeded to the school entrance to see if anyone was coming to school, as surely the whole school could not be late altogether. The sight of the whole junior school perched like a row of birds at roost greeted him. Thinking that the children had misjudged the time he beckoned them into the school. He was then astounded by the reply that came back, 'Sorry, sir, we have gone on strike'. Having no recollection of this being covered at Teacher Training College, his solution was to pass the problem to the Headmaster.

The sight of the Headmaster, Mr Sammy Taylor, had an immediate effect, he being a man of stern qualities who would brook no

Blue Coat Junior School. (Picture sent in by Wendy Hodson).

nonsense. Gradually, the pupils jumped down off the fence and filtered sheepishly past the glowering headmaster, with the sole exception of two of the tougher Ryecroft lads – Inskip and Evans. When approached by Sammy Taylor, the two remaining strikers decided to run for it, leaving the Headmaster stranded and breathless. They were last seen heading across the Sandhole towards their native Ryecroft. Meanwhile, the school settled down to the usual routine in the various classes. Each teacher and class carried on as normal until the bell rang for the end of school. Thankfully the pupils hastily made their way home, having at least expected to be detained after hours, with possibly lines to write out.

After a good night's sleep the pupils returned to the school the following morning and gathered around in groups, speculating on what would happen to the two truants. The truants arrived just prior to the morning bell for assembly and, being of the harder type, affected not to care less about the previous afternoon's exploits. It was the school custom and routine in those pre First World War days for the whole school to assemble in the main hall for morning prayers, each master or mistress taking it in turns to deliver a short sermon. This morning, in particular, the various classes were surprised by the Headmaster performing the said duty seemingly in an oppressive mood.

After the prayers were over there was a pause that seemed to last for hours, and instead of the customary file into the respective classrooms came a stern booming request from the Headmaster. 'Come out to the front of the school Lieutenant Evans and Colonel Inskip'. This they did, only to see the Headmaster produce the school tawse from behind the hall desk. He then pronounced 'It was your turn to strike yesterday, so it's my turn to strike today, lads'. They were ordered to bend over a conveniently placed bench to receive probably the most ferocious thrashing in the annals of North Walsall's junior school. So, with very sore backsides, the rebels rejoined the ranks of silent pupils to remember this event for many years, but I doubt that many of them who have now passed on would have visualized it being remembered and retold now in 2002.

This was remembered some years ago by ex pupil Walter Franklin and confirmed by Ray Wilson. Confirmation of the thrashing was found by J. Haddock in the logbook of the school for 1911.

Jack Haddock

Willow House School

I was born in 1934 and I attended Pelsall Lane Infants and Junior School. During my junior school days I was attending an eye infirmary at Wolverhampton two days a week, so my primary schooling was a bit sketchy. I failed the Eleven Plus and rather than attend Shelfield School I was sent to Willow House School, Wednesbury Road, Walsall.

The establishment consisted of a single, large room at the rear of Mr Hughes' house. You passed the house and the short garden and entered through a small vestibule where we hung our maroon jackets and hats and entered the schoolroom, which had a cast iron stove set in the centre. Mr Douglas Hughes was middle aged, old to us; he must have been in his fifties and had a long, wide centre parting. He was the sole teacher and controlled forty boys in the age range six to sixteen. We sat at long desks, four and five in a row, and there were four double desks for the prefects.

Everyone sat facing the windows on a long wall to the right and a little space was left for access between the desks and benches. 'Dougy' Hughes' desk was in the centre of the longer wall on the left-hand side, on a wooden dais looking at our backs. The benches had no backs, so if he wished to chalk on the blackboard or communicate a subject, we could turn around and lean against our desks. Also, of course, when we opened our desks he could see straight inside.

The school was noted for the style of handwriting, a formal script, thick and thin strokes. Left-handed people were not tolerated: 'You write thus and thus'. The tip of the steel nib pen points to your shoulder. Your wrist is flat on the paper. The down strokes are straight and have a little pressure to make them thick. It did make your wrist ache at first but quickly the style came, and then the fingers became used to the writing position. You only had to lapse for a moment and Dougy would be behind you with a quick flick on your knuckles with his extended 'pen holder'; a thin cane about a foot long, which he kept up his sleeve. You knew you had strayed and the flick was taken in the same attitude as it was given, a reminder, sore for a moment.

Dougy had assistance for two mornings a week from an equally aged fellow whose nose twitched like a rabbit's. Mr Sandy, 'Bunny' Sandy to us low life. He taught the lower forms on the other side of a five-foot folding screen, which was placed across the centre of the room from time to time. One afternoon a week. a lady came to teach us French. I can't remember her name. She introduced a textbook and opened it at page one. By the end of the term the upper forms had memorized the first five or six exercises: the garden; the dining room; numbers; time and greetings. The next term introduced a few new boys from the lower forms, so we started again page one – we never did go to the exhibition in exercise seven.

Names I recall from that time are: Adams, Hawker, Tame, Clarridge, Hodson, Burton, Thorp, Bird, Stanton, Fletcher, Skidmore. Who blew the tip off his thumb with fireworks? Barnes, that was the boy!

I wonder who turned off the water to the boys' toilet one summer weekend and the place was full of flies after half term.

The routine for the day started with the reading of a Psalm, each boy in turn, starting with the head boy, read a verse and the School said the second and so on. We abbreviated CXIX into about thirty verses, starting 'Blessed are the undefiled'; finishing at the last verse 178, ' I have gone astray like a lost sheep'. Then we had the Lord's Prayer.

Mondays and Wednesdays the first period was Maths; Tuesdays and Thursdays Algebra; Fridays Euclid. The rest of the week passed, except Wednesdays, when after lunch the first period was Dictation, mostly read from Dickens, the funny bits. Once you had copied out your spelling mistakes twenty times each, you could attend gym or games. Thursday afternoon was Art. Dougy would produce a bunch of wild flowers and drop a few onto each desk. For these sessions the whole school came together. The gym equipment was stored against the wall behind the cloakrooms, with the coconut mats rolled up in the parallel bars. The rings were hoisted up to the ceiling. Dougy was quite nimble; I think he would practice in the evenings.

I mentioned lunch. Most of the boys were local or at most a bus ride away in Wednesbury, Darlaston or Rushall. On occasions we took our lunch in the 'British Restaurant' in Dale Street. At the end of my period at school the restaurant had moved to Little Newport Street.

We had no playing field as such but for a kick about there was the fairground site in Midland Road, just a black ash area, which matched our knees.

At other times, for instance the severe winter days when very few of the pupils turned up, Dougy would find his ventriloquist's dummy, Elmore Snodgrass, and pass an hour away until it was reasonable to send us home.

Mr Hughes received a lengthy obituary in the *Walsall Observer* when he died in the 1960s, which account would be much more accurate than my ramblings! I do understand, however, that he attended Durham University where he studied Music and Maths and that he was a fine organist, playing at St Paul's church. Upon receiving his degree he joined Lloyd's Bank and placed a number of boys from Willow House there. He must have made an impression at the branch, for quite quickly he was moved to Birmingham, Colmore Row. The strain was too much and he suffered a breakdown. To recuperate he was found work at a farm somewhere near Slimbridge. His knowledge of natural history was legendary and his sketches and watercolours hung everywhere.

Later he joined the Walsall Police and became Chief Constable. He would bring his decorated truncheon to the schoolroom sometimes. I can only surmise that upon the death of his father, who founded the school, Douglas Hughes took up the reins of Willow House.

To go home every day, after the Grace had been said, Dougy would start a quiz, general knowledge, but in the main mental arithmetic: What is the price of a gross of apples at three halfpence each? Multiply 345 by 25! This limited the number of boys let loose into the Wednesbury Road at any one time.

It was a gentle life. Little homework was set unless you had a weak subject. At the end we all said goodbye to Douglas Hughes and his wife, trailed along the garden path to the granite step and down onto the pavement for a bus to town. At this point I realized I knew nothing that would earn me a living. Mr Hughes gave us all he had. He showed the boys a route and thirst to know more, a realization that this step on the edge of the Wednesbury Road was the new life. I had to get some different education!

Brian Griffiths

8th June, 1946

TO-DAY, AS WE CELEBRATE VICTORY, I send this personal message to you and all other boys and girls at school. For you have shared in the hardships and dangers of a total war and you have shared no less in the triumph of the Allied Nations.

I know you will always feel proud to belong to a country which was capable of such supreme effort; proud, too, of parents and elder brothers and sisters who by their courage, endurance and enterprise brought victory. May these qualities be yours as you grow up and join in the common effort to establish among the nations of the world unity and peace.

George R.I

Message from King George VI dated 6 June 1946, given to schoolchildren after the war.

Schooldays of yesteryear

I owe a very great deal to Walsall, where I was born and where I lived and worked for the first fifty years of my life.

In the 1930s I remember being rowed by my father on the Arboretum Lake – so deliciously dangerous because it was said to be bottomless – and then going further into the park to see the peacocks and the glasshouses.

I recall the National School in Bloxwich, which I loved. There was such a handsome smiling policeman to see us children across the High Street after school. The headmistress could be fearsome at times; I remember her at morning assembly writing on the blackboard 'CLEAN YOUR BOOTS' among different daily slogans. She kept the 'rough boys' under tight control, occasionally resorting to 'the strap' on a child's outstretched hand. All the same she was very kind when she needed to be. We had a party for George Vs Jubilee, when we had jelly, cake and games. I had a new frock with red, white and blue round the hem and we primary school children were each given a commemorative mug.

When my mother was young, at the beginning of the twentieth century, she went to Bluecoat School which was then on the Bridge. She told us she used to run all the way down the hill from her home in Hanch Place near St Matthew's church so as not to be late for school. Discipline was strictly enforced and the children were rapped on the knuckles with a ruler, or punished with the leather tawse. Empire Day, which I believe was on 24 May, was celebrated every year, usually by a pageant when the children dressed up as natives of the many countries of the Empire, with someone as Britannia. Later mother went to Queen Mary's High School; so did I, and so did my daughter.

When it was time for my class to leave the junior National School, some of my classmates moved to the senior department. Several went to Elmore Green School which concentrated on a commercial training and a number of others were transferred at thirteen to the Walsall Technical College, afterwards to become apprentices and to gain national certificates in such subjects as engineering or building.

I passed the scholarship and started at Queen Mary's in 1940, and have vivid memories of wartime life there – though of course we girls took all the shortages and restrictions in our stride, never having been conscious of any other way of life. The Depression and unemployment in the 1930s meant that the standard of living was low for most of us. Queen Mary's rules about uniform had to be relaxed in wartime, but only slightly; there was a good supply of second-hand uniforms available at low cost. We were not allowed to be seen in the street without our 'tams' (woollen berets in the school colours of red, yellow and green). Stockings or ankle-socks had to be worn at all times, much to our chagrin because in the summer we did so want to get our legs brown with no white areas at the ankles! In the street we were not allowed to eat anything or walk more than two abreast. If a teacher or prefect saw you transgressing you might lose your deportment badge!

School dinners provided a welcome addition to the rations on which our mothers were trying to feed us. Spam seemed delicious to us when it started to come though from the USA – we had not had anything so tasty for years! It was certainly more popular than marrow in cheese sauce, which was a standby when there was nothing else to be had.

Practice air-raid drills provided an occasional diversion from lessons, but it was really not that much fun being herded into the underground shelters which were dank, dark dismal places that became very stuffy. I don't remember any real raids during school hours. 6 June 1944 I will always remember, of course. Our geography teacher, Miss Beecroft,

Elmore Green Central School.

got out a map of the English Channel and impressed us with the huge importance of the Allied landings in Normandy that morning.

We were occasionally allowed to help 'Dig for Victory' in the garden at Mayfield, the then junior department of Queen Mary's. Picking raspberries was the best part of that.

The slogans 'Is your journey really necessary?' and 'Holidays at Home' were seen everywhere. The only school trip I remember was one to Cambridge for a week to pick plums for the Chivers jam factory. We took our bikes on the train, as they were essential to get to the orchards. Some local ladies made up beds in the nearby school and fed us well. We had great fun climbing ladders, singing and even earning some pocket money. Cambridge was as far as some of us ever got from Walsall.

One of the nicest things about school in those days was break-time (times have not changed in this respect, anyway). We were allowed to play dance records and do quicksteps, waltzes, foxtrots and so on. Sometimes we each paid 3d for the privilege of a longer dance break, to raise money for Spitfire or Warship week. There was a Hollier's shop in Lichfield Street, which provided trays of lovely buns for us to buy. I particularly liked their Shrewsbury biscuits. I don't know how they managed to keep up the standard they did.

We made our way into the town when school finished for the day. Many of us caught one of the trolley buses, which turned round at the Bridge. There was not much room to spare there because of the enormous circular water tank which had to be kept full in case the fire service could not obtain water from the mains in a raid. Walsall was grimy as resources were kept for more important things than cleaning buildings. Today's Walsall residents would not recognize the black town hall of those days.

Many of our teachers had to defer retirement because the Services and other war work occupied a large proportion of younger people, but Miss Stafford was an inspirational Head. During morning assembly she had a knack of giving us something to think about which was to stay with us for life. She and the other staff gave us a wonderful education, which has certainly enabled us to appreciate and benefit from so many aspects of the world we live in and has enriched our lives.

Thank you, Walsall

Josie Fenton

An inauspicious start to a new era

A History of Beacon Primary School

Newspaper reports of 1951 told of the desperate overcrowding that New Invention Primary School was suffering. The new Beacon Colliery Estate was nearing completion and several families moved into their new homes during the school holidays, with the result that 350 children turned up for school when it re-opened after the summer holiday.

With a maximum capacity of 250, the Headteacher, Mr Evans, faced the nightmare situation of accommodating an extra 100 children. The housing on Beacon Colliery Estate may have been nearing completion, but the new school was still very much 'under construction' and labour shortage and 'other difficulties' meant completion was still some distance away.

A piecemeal solution to this problem was found when children were accommodated anywhere space could be found. Some schools helped by providing space for one class, another Head insisted that any pupils coming to his school became pupils of his school and would not allow temporary accommodation to pupils from somewhere else. One class was actually housed in the new buildings from 1951, but it was to be some time before the rest joined them.

After an approach from the school managers, Reverend W.D. Hopkinson, vicar of Short Heath, agreed to allow the extra pupils to be accommodated in the old church school buildings, which themselves had been condemned as unsuitable for school use some twenty-five years previously!

Clearly this accommodation was unsuitable on a long-term basis. The buildings were used for other purposes and these uses were to continue during the occupation by the school children. The parish meetings, weekly clinic, rates collections, dances, concerts and other functions all went ahead regardless. Friday afternoons proved particularly difficult as a clinic was held in the school, meaning that girls were sent to the main school for needlework and boys had to undergo outdoor PE for the afternoon.

It was September 1952 before the new Beacon Colliery School opened, meaning the children due to attend this school had to endure the whole winter in grim conditions, using buildings that were deemed unsuitable for their parents, or even grandparents! Although completion of the building had been delayed, the urgency had not been anticipated as families were moved in to the new houses on the estate. School places were normally allocated on the basis of 1.5 places per family, yet some of the new families were moving onto the estate with up to fifteen school age children.

Finally the new school opened in nearly completed buildings that won an architectural award. Beacon County Primary School was born. Actually, the new baby was a twin – two schools but just one Head to begin with. Mr Bill Pearson took charge of the junior school. After a further twelve months a second Head – Miss Algar - was appointed to the Infants School and the two schools began their separate histories, Beacon Junior School and Beacon Infant School respectively.

The word 'Colliery' was dropped from the name before opening and now the pit seems long forgotten. At the time of opening it was hardly forgotten, though, as a pit mound remained next to the building awaiting flattening and seeding to create the school playing field. The sense of urgency was keenly felt as final touches were put to the school. Perhaps a little too much urgency as the bulldozer driver undertook too ambitious a cut out of the mound and had several tons of earth collapse on top of him. He was dug from the scene by frantic workmates and taken to hospital where, thankfully, he discovered his injuries were not too serious.

The school was still not complete when the first classes were moved into the buildings. The end of the school where the dining rooms and halls now stand was still little more than a skeleton as children moved into classrooms at the further end of the corridor, having access to the doors in and out of the Junior playground. Access was available just as far as the girls' toilets.

A relief to all, especially the boy who arrived at school one wet morning covered in mud from head to toe, and had to spend the morning cleaning himself up. When Mr Pearson made inquiries into the reason for him arriving in such a state, he was told 'Frank pushed me in the drainage trench on Jones Road.' The work to complete the estate was still in progress. When asked why he had pushed the boy into the drainage trench, Frank explained quite reasonably that he wanted to find out how deep the trench was. A little deeper than the height of one small boy, apparently. This was in the days when children learned the Imperial method of measurement – two chains, one pole; four poles, one furlong; eight furlongs, one mile; two small boys, one drainage trench.

The official opening ceremony took place on 7 October 1953. Lord Lieutenant of Staffordshire, H. Wallace-Copland Esq. JP performed the ceremony before several specially invited guests were entertained by the school choir and allowed to tour the school to inspect the long-awaited newly completed buildings.

Once the school had been open for a little while and had had a chance to settle and establish its own ethos, inevitably it began to attract the attention of the School Inspectors who always like to cast an eye over the progress of a new school. Sure enough one Mr Doubleday turned up to put the teachers and pupils through their paces. After a morning of listening to carefully prepared responses and 'pat' lessons, he decided it would be more revealing to eat with the children at dinnertime to get a real view of what the school was like. Many of the children were a little shy of sitting with the 'School Spectre', but Frank was chosen as the right person to chaperone him. He chatted away answering questions readily. When the conversation got round to what he had been doing in his spare time out of school, Mr Doubleday realized his error. He was treated to graphic descriptions of Frank catching frogs, starting a fire, filling a can with water and boiling up the frogs! Enough to put off even the most strong-stomached inspector from his dinner.

Both schools thrived for several years with long-serving heads establishing the mould for each. Mrs Nora Worsnop replaced Miss Algar as Head of the Infants. In 1970 a nursery was added, accommodated by roofing over a quadrangle and converting a cloakroom. Many parents and grandparents will have fond memories of Beryl Nicklin who worked in the Nursery from its very early stages until her retirement in July 2002.

Staff came and went over the years, too many to allow for individual mention of many, but lots of local families will tell tales of life under the leadership of Mr Pearson in the Junior school, or Mrs Worsnop in the Infants. In 1974 Lynn Thomas became the second Headteacher of the junior school and stayed until 1978 when Tony Critchley took over. Liz Tubb continued the work Nora Worsnop had started in the Infants school until her retirement in 1999.

Following the death of Bill Pearson in December 1978, the Junior school instituted a special award in his memory. Each year the child in Year Six who is judged by the whole staff – secretaries, dinner ladies, teachers – to have made the most significant contribution to the school is awarded the Pearson Award. It is a respectful way to honour both a well-respected Head and a pupil showing considerable character.

The large field that backs on to the school has been the centre of many local events as well as sports days, fêtes and games lessons. The tale is still told of the Deputy Head who would referee a football match from an upstairs classroom window if the weather were at all inclement!

Stories also abound of the ghost, which haunts the school. Children are often afraid to go to the back of the upstairs hall alone for fear of the ghost of the former school caretaker who lurks below the stage waiting to grab unsuspecting children and drag them off to his lair. The truth of the story is rather more prosaic. The caretaker at the time, Mr Jackson, collapsed and died in the school, his body discovered by two pupils out of class acting as milk monitors.

In 1999, Mrs Liz Gratwick (formerly Mrs Tubb) retired and the decision was taken to amalgamate the two schools. Beacon Junior School and Beacon Infant School were both officially closed down and a new school opened in their place – Beacon Primary School. The new Head of the new school was Tony Critchley who had already spent over twenty years as Head of the Junior School.

He took on the sometimes tricky role of establishing the new school and merging the ethos of both previous schools into a single new one, until his retirement in December 2000 when he was replaced by Mrs Donna Wharton who is guiding the school into its next era. We were particularly proud to open an art gallery in the junior corridor in November 2001, thanks to sponsorship from Natwest Bank. Work by children of all ages throughout the school is on display along with samples of work by former pupils, teachers and friends of the school.

So in the year of the Golden Jubilee of Queen Elizabeth II, Beacon Primary School also celebrates its fiftieth anniversary. Our own Golden Jubilee saw the school doors opened to visitors who have had connections with the school during its history. A large contingent of former teachers, dinner ladies, pupils and friends toured the school. A 1950s style school dinner was served up, to the surprising delight of many pupils past and present, but at 2002 prices, unfortunately. The pupils were subjected to a day of 1950s style lessons, and some actually appreciated the formality, although few managed to dress in authentic style. Thankfully, the week of celebrations reached a peak with the 'street party' held in the playground where all the pupils were treated to food, music and games; giant tug-of-war competitions rounded off the memorable occasion.

Several photographs exist in the school archive of staff and children at various points in the school's history. If you feel like checking up on old friends, or want to be sure that you really did wear that jumper, then take a look at the school's website – www.beacon.walsall.sch.uk.

James Moffat

My Experiences at Sandwell School

Bright and gaudy were two words I would use to describe our school blazers. Their maroon fabric was edged with shiny gold braid, making them visible half a mile away and the gold embroidered badge on the top pocket added to the glare. Although the first blazer I had was plain maroon without the braid. Why the gold addition was made, I can't imagine!

In the winter the girls also wore a navy, box-pleated gym-slip, blouse, striped school tie and velour hat complete with ribbon and sheering elastic, to hold it on our heads and in the cold and wet weather, a heavy-weight gabardine raincoat. We all carried leather satchels of differing sizes, shades and shapes.

This is how I looked as a young pupil of Sandwell School, Streetly. Underneath the gymslip were, hopefully unseen, a liberty bodice which anchored stockings in place, the inevitable vest and baggy maroon knickers (yuck!).

Situated in Blackwood Road, the school premises consisted of a pair of semi-detached houses, which were used by the younger children for lessons, a row of purpose-built classrooms and the school hall which overlooked the playground to the rear of the houses. On the far side of the playgroup were the bike sheds where boys hid and smoked. An area for tennis courts extended almost as far as Foley Road West.

Prior to starting at the school as an infant, Mum and Dad took me to the bungalow in Streetly of Mr R.A.F. Newton-Herne, the headmaster and owner of the school. There we were interviewed and I was accepted as a pupil. As this was a private school, Dad had to pay a fee for me to attend but I have no idea how much that figure was.

When I started, with my new uniform properly marked with Cashes' nametapes (they were red on white so that everything would be co-ordinated), I found that there were fewer girls than there were boys. My class friends were Angela Webb, Leslie Kibble, Fiona Lamont and Jane Vincent and we sat together – away from the boys. All pupils were allocated to houses when they first arrived and I was in Tudor house and so, in due course, was my younger brother David. We were identified by our green badges. The pupils allocated to other houses sported different colours; Lancaster had yellow and Windsor had red.

Classroom in the infant section showing Anne Nicklin, by the fireplace in front of the teacher.

Mr Newton-Herne, or the Beak as we knew him, always tried to maintain an air of hard work and an ethos of honour and good manners at the school. Our school motto was *Alteri sic tibi* which, we were frequently told, meant we should do to others the things we would like done to us. We liked to change the words to 'Alter sick tabby'. Mr Newton-Herne would have been furious, had he known.

Discipline was important and we knew naughty children would be punished and, for an extreme misdemeanour, expelled. It was the boys who were physically punished as it would not have been gentlemanly to hit a girl, so I don't think it was ever considered. Any boy who had severely misbehaved was sent to the Beak's study for the cane or 'six of the best'. Otherwise there was a rap on the knuckles with a rule or lines had to be written out. One boy, I think it was Roger Nabb, had to write one hundred lines 'I must call a potato a potato' when a teacher caught him using the word 'spud'. I had to write several words, which I had spelt incorrectly, a hundred times. It did not help, as I still can't spell!

Lessons were on the whole enjoyable. The form teachers, most of whom wore gowns, used to call register in the morning: boys were addressed by their surnames and girls by their Christian names. We would answer 'Here' in response to our name. Then lessons would commence. I liked the art teacher, Mr Green, who painted a watercolour of a bonfire with bright orange and red flames and he used some of my black paint for the contrasting wood at the bottom. I was so impressed!

For French, we had a real M'selle who tried to teach us her language and improve our French grammar. There was confusion about whether people should be addressed in the second person singular and whether it translated as 'you' or 'thou'. Despite her help, my French did not develop very quickly. Another teacher, Reverend Cartmel, I had mixed feelings about. He would tell us Scripture stories and tales of his own experiences, which were fascinating but I hated it when he called me out in front of the class. He would hold my plaits round the back of my neck and keep me there. I must have been one of his favourites but it was uncomfortable just the same.

I loved the woods at the end of Blackwood Road. If the weather was fine and the teacher allowed we would walk up there and find a place to sit for our lessons. It was there I saw, for the first time, a Great Spotted woodpecker and heard the tap-tap of its beak against a tree trunk. We could draw and learn about nature at first hand in the pleasant atmosphere. The boys would run 'cross-country' around the woods and we girls would cheer them on.

As long as everyone behaved, the atmosphere was pleasant. However, one event sticks in my mind clearly. The Beak arrived in assembly with his gown flowing higher than usual and holding a filthy dirty roller towel for all to see. This, he announced, had come from the boys' toilets that had been left in a disgraceful state. We then had a graphic description of the mess.

The toilet block was situated at the far side of the playground from the hall and main classrooms and the girls' side was cold and basic and we were supplied with one clean towel. I imagine that the boys' side was similar, but there were many more of them using the spartan facility.

Anyway, the Beak continued with our telling off. We were expected to behave as gentlemen and gentlewomen – he used this word a lot and I thought he had not heard of the word 'lady'. By the end of his condemnation of the boys and the way they behaved, I too was feeling uncomfortable. I think one of the boys must have cleaned the mud off his shoes on the towel. I am sure he would not do it again.

During the summer term the girls wore red check dresses with the blazers and I even had a red gingham handkerchief to match my dress. It was at this time that we used the school field in Wood Lane for athletics. Sporting activities were an important aspect of life at Sandwell School and everyone was expected to join in. On our sports day, the boys competed for a *Victor Laudorum* trophy and the most successful girl for the *Victrix Laudorum* or was it *Laudora* – my Latin was no good either!

'It's not the winning that is important, it's the taking part!' we were so often told. So we would leave the school for the short walk to Wood Lane in a glaringly obvious uniform. The field was marked out into a running track and the inadequately mown grass had spiky bits that kept sticking into your legs and then there were small pebbles to hinder your running. I was just involved in the taking part and not in the winning.

Once the energetic parts were out of the way and we had eaten the food provided by some of the mothers in the wooden pavilion, we could let off steam and enjoy ourselves.

I can't remember us going to the field during the winter but we were generally taught games in the playground. There were tennis and netball courts for us to use in lesson time.

At break time, we used this area for play; 'tig' was popular or we played hopscotch or skipped. In particular, we skipped with a long rope with someone holding each end. They would turn the rope and we would run in and out in turn and count the number of skips we could do. Often two or three girls would run in together, we would hop over the rope on one leg or we would see who could skip the fastest. One of my favourites was:

Here we go together, girls,
This fine weather, girls,
When I call your birthday,
Please run out - January, February, March…

In this game we all skipped together, then as the month of your birthday came, you had to run out.

Generally, break times were spent outside but when it was really cold or wet we had to remain indoors. We girls would chat together amongst ourselves. It was on one of these occasions that Jane Vincent told us where babies come from. I was horrified to think that they came out of your Mummy's tummy, which would split open along the line down from her belly button. This information was imparted with great secrecy and it was some time before I learned more accurately what happened in childbirth.

While I attended the school, I had elocution lessons. Only a few pupils came from the Walsall area where vowels are not pronounced as Mrs Newton-Herne liked. My diction was considered to be common but I did not want to speak as if I had a plum in my mouth so I expect that is why my progress was so slow. Many of my friends came from Sutton Coldfield or Birmingham, so did not have the same problem as I did.

When David started school, I would go and collect him from his classroom. Often he would leave his shoelaces undone and I would help teach him to tie them and assist him on with his coat. When others would want to pick a fight, there I was to defend him. It is surprising how quickly I slipped into the mothering role.

David and I travelled to school on the bus with one of the teachers, Mrs Brookes who lived a few houses away from us on the Sutton Road. We used to stand and wait on the island by Longwood Lane: a spot exposed to wind, snow and rain. My Wellingtons kept the wet out but my feet were often numb with the cold, so then I would get chilblains. If there had been a heavy fall of snow, the buses did not go over Barr Beacon Hill, which meant we would have to walk. On the days when it was really deep, we walked both ways.

David and Anne Nicklin.

We were expected to behave properly while on the bus, not like the 'Council Kids' who attended the school on Foley Road West and who shouted and threw things at us. They called us the 'Sandwell Snobs' which I expect we were, partly due to the strong reminders we were given that we were representatives of the school. Its honour was in our hands! Not that we never threw anything back: we did it when no teacher was looking.

One day, Fiona and I were waiting at the bus stop to go home when a black saloon car stopped and the driver leaned over and asked if we would like to see his kittens. I would have gone with him but Fiona said that we were waiting for her mother who was going to meet us. So he drove off. I had no idea it was wrong or dangerous to get into a car like that.

Overall I enjoyed my years at Sandwell School. I left in 1954 to attend Queen Mary's in Walsall, after passing the Eleven Plus. Especially, I remember the comradeship: the pulling together for the good of the school or the house. I like to think that my concept of honour was born at Sandwell and I am thankful for the good basis of general education I received there.

Anne James

Eighteen months at St Patrick's School, Walsall in the mid-1930s

I was born in September 1929 in Rushall. When I was nearing my seventh birthday my paternal grandmother died. My grandfather would not live by himself or move in with us so my parents had no alternative but rent out our home and move in with him in Walsall.

Consequently, in September 1936, instead of returning to my school in Shelfield after the summer break, I found myself starting at St Patrick's in Blue Lane, Walsall. I settled in quickly, soon making many friends, including Sally Kelly and Louie Diccicio.

My teachers were Sister Agnes and Miss Humphries and Miss Egan. I remember each with great fondness – they were kind and made me feel very welcome at the school. I enjoyed all my studies, particularly essay writing – one of my favourites being the Life of Sister Dora. I even rather enjoyed needlework – something I had hated before.

My journey to school was always interesting. When I first started I was escorted by my cousin Leo who was five years older than me. Leo and I would dash past the Wolverhampton Road schools to avoid taunting children. We would then sometimes linger outside the flourmill watching the bags of flour being hauled up through trap doors.

Sometimes I would take an alternative route to school through the Birchills and I would stay to watch the men working in red-hot conditions in the iron foundry.

Towards Christmas of that year I attended Sunday Mass as usual when, to my amazement, when mass was over, most of the children, including some of my friends, crossed over the road and stood in line outside the Presbytery. I joined them but had not stood for many seconds before Father McDonnell, who was the Parish Priest, came and removed me from my friends saying, 'What on earth are you doing here?'

Just as I moved away I recognized the figure of Pat Collins moving towards the head of the line of children. He then proceeded to hand each child a brown paper bag. I watched this mortified, wondering why I was not allowed one of these bags. By this time my embarrassed parents had reached my side, my mother asking me what on earth had possessed me to join the children in the first place.

It appeared that Pat Collins gave fatherless children, or children whose fathers were out of work (remember this was 1936) a bag each containing fruit and other goods. As both my father and grandfather were working, I obviously did not qualify, but at the time I was most upset.

Father McDonnell sadly died whilst I was at St Patrick's. I remember us children being taken to the Presbytery class by class to pay our respects to the open coffin.

I was still a pupil at St Patrick's in May 1937 at the time of the Coronation of King George VI and Queen Elizabeth. Unfortunately just beforehand I was taken ill with a bad attack of measles so could not attend either the party at school or join in the street party where we lived.

On the actual day of the Coronation I was up and about again but my mother was very conscious of the fact that I could still be contagious so would not let me near other children. This disappointed me a great deal but my father had a brain wave. He bundled my mum and me into the car and drove us around as many of the streets of Walsall as he could, showing us the decorations and all the street parties so I felt I had not missed out altogether.

During my time at St Patrick's I remember the wonderful pantomimes Father McDonnell, the nuns and teachers worked so hard to produce and put on at the church hall in Stafford Street. I appeared as one of the flames of the lamp in *Aladdin*. One of my aunties said at the time that not one of us small children had a tooth left in our heads. I don't know how true that was.

Fancy dress parties were also held in St Patrick's hall about November time. I did win one prize in 1937 dressed as a Dutch girl. I still treasure my prize, *Alice in Wonderland*, after over sixty years. At the same competition in 1937 my cousin Leo, dressed as Simple Simon, won an

St Patrick's Roman Catholic School.

illuminated watch. This was a real novelty in 1937 and the prize mesmerized us children.

I enjoyed my time at St Patrick's School very much but life at home with my grandfather was another story. Let us just say that when he informed us he was getting married again we could not leave his home fast enough, so 1938 saw me returning to my original school, St Francis of Assisi in Shelfield.

Margaret Cooper

9 Local Characters

The outdoor beer licence at 135, Bloxwich Road, North Walsall

From 1930 until 1960, a Mr Joseph Venables owned this off licence establishment. The shop was also a grocery shop open seven days a week for beer and spirits and six days for groceries, opening at 8 a.m. and closing at 10 p.m. One could purchase bottled beer, which could be taken in stone jars or empty pop bottles but at no time could a person drink on the premises. The same applied to spirits. For beer and spirits the opening hours were 12.00 noon until 2 p.m. and 6 p.m. until 10 p.m. For groceries the shop would sell from 8 a.m. until 6 p.m. Sunday hours were the same, although no groceries could be sold on Sundays.

Upon entering the shop one was immediately struck by the immaculate display and cleanliness. On the numerous shelves and stands were a vast number of bottled beers, stout and spirits, including a range of various brands of pop. Joe arranged all these bottles in rows that were as precise and straight as a company of well-drilled soldiers. The same applied to the window display. Near the doorway was a stack of empty beer and pop crates in which customers deposited their empties before a fresh purchase. After about five crates became full, Joe would find time to move them to the rear yard so as not to appear unsightly. To the rear of the shop the shelves in the grocery department were also very tidy and neat. A screen hid the bacon slicer from view.

For both beer and grocery trade, Joe Venables, through his personality and efficiency, acquired many regular customers near North Walsall. My family and many others worked to a system of the housewife making up an order book in mid-week of one week's requirements, including the basic needs like butter, tea, sugar, bacon, tinned fruit etc. They would deposit the book with Joe Venables, who would on Friday or Saturday have the contents ready in a brown paper parcel, wrapped with string and order book attached with the amount of cash to be paid. Thus housewives, whose husbands were paid at the weekends, could settle. Housewives in that era would plan for one week's food supply (not like today, when people run to the shops many times per day, with no organized plan). For a sum of 1s, Joe had a delivery cycle and a regular lad to deliver the week's grocery. The sum the lad was paid was 6d for each delivery, so local lads made good earnings on this part time job.

Joe would do a very brisk trade with the beer, especially during the evenings. His wife, who was dressed as immaculately as Joe, would always appear in the shop as trade increased. A ritual among the local working class residents was for husbands and wives to enjoy their beer at home, incorporating cheese and onion sandwiches to finish the day. Us children were allowed to fetch draft beer in surplus two pint pop bottles. Each child's purchase would have a special seal placed over the cork to the bottle side. This procedure was law for children under eighteen years and Joe Venables ensured no child left his shop without a sealed bottle. If a passing police officer saw a child carrying an unsealed beer bottle, an off licence could lose its licence. It did not go unnoticed during the opening midday opening hours that a few local housewives found time to nip down to the beer licence for dinnertime refreshment when their husbands were at work and their children at school. I am not a drinking man but I recollect that the draught beer sold at North Walsall Off Licence was Highgate Ale, brewed at Walsall's local brewery, a mild ale and old ale, a strong brew that appealed to the working man. Most of the bottled beer was the product of Mitchells and Butlers. Their nourishing stout was popular with the women, as was Guinness stout. An amusing memory of this era was, that during the influenza epidemic, my father would try the following cure that was practised by a lot of working men: I would be sent to the beer licence for one quart of old ale and to purchase a small amount of ginger powder. On arrival back home my father would have the coal fire hot, with the poker inserted into the hot coals until glowing red-hot. A pint glass would then be filled with old ale and generous helpings of ginger. The red-hot poker was thrust into the beer with much fizz and gurgling and the hot beer then consumed. It was supposed to cure flu and colds but it appears today that no process has been made to cure even the common cold. It does not seem that my father's contribution to this medical dilemma made any difference.

Sunday night visits to the outdoor beer licence were, to say the least, different. Joe Venables was a lover of classical music and had an extension loud speaker attached into the shop from the household wireless. His favourite programme on Sunday evenings was the broadcast from the Grand Hotel of the Palm Court Orchestra, with the famous violinist Albert Sandler. The look of ecstasy on Joe's face whilst operating the beer pulls had to be seen to be believed. I often suggested some dance band music to liven up the evening but Joe gave a reply that such music was the work of the devil. At the mention of jazz, Joe would point to the door, but only after he had served you! With these verbal fisticuffs, Joe sported a light smile. Many years later I was serving in the Royal Air Force as a driver on the South Coast Radar Chain, occasional duties included chauffeuring senior officers to various hotels. These duties took me to the Grand Hotel where my task was to help them with their luggage into the hotel. On one occasion I passed the sun lounge where Albert Sandler was playing to an assortment of well off retired people. When on leave I visited Joe Venables to remark that I had seen his idol, but he never believed me.

When the Second World War began, Joe Venables was over military age. This meant that the beer licence and grocery shop would remain open. With the advent of food rationing, our family had no hesitation in registering with Joe for groceries. Being a very fair and efficient shopkeeper Joe had quite a considerable list of customers. During the 1940-1942 period, a time of great uncertainty, beer and cigarettes became scarce. It was to Joe's credit that he looked after his regular customers. At no time was there any friction or discontent. America came into the war in properly in 1942 and later in 1943 we began to enjoy the luxury of tinned fruit and Spam, with each customer receiving their allotted ration. Besides running the off licence, during the war Joe found time to assist in Air Raid Precaution duties in the North Walsall ARP post opposite the shop. Joe was well past military age during the war. Joe and his wife never had a holiday together during his thirty years in North Walsall Off Licence. Separate holidays of one week only a year were the rule. His wife, who was an exceptionally good-looking woman, was more than capable of running the business. It so happened that she had two good-looking sisters married to local shopkeepers, one in nearby Gladstone Street running a grocery shop and the other a general store in Bloxwich Road near Pratts Bridge, dealing with charging accumulators for the primitive battery wireless of that era.

After the war I did not see Joe, owing to my five years in HM Forces. His departure and retirement were practically unnoticed. Joe Venables retired to Blackpool where some local North Walsall customers came across Joe working as a deck chair attendant. This was typical of Joe, whose philosophy of life was to be always active. They remarked how fit he was, then in his late sixties. After some years at Blackpool, Joe and his wife retired to Bournemouth to spend his last days. Looking back it was a privilege to be associated with Joe Venables and his wife.

Jack Haddock

The Man in the barrel

Many of the residents of Walsall and surrounding areas will recall the 'man in a barrel' also referred to as the 'man up the pole'. Those who are younger may well have heard the story. Vic Reeves was just twenty-three years old when he took on a wager made by Mr. Claude Roe, local restaurateur and proprietor of the New Yorker restaurant in Walsall. Never one to turn down a dare he agreed to stay in a barrel long enough to break the world record. The barrel measured just 31/2ft high and 2ft 4ins across and was hoisted and secured to the top of a pole 40ft above the ground.

The first Vic's wife, Beryl, heard of it was when she was told to come and look at the pole only to see her husband in the process of scrambling up the final feet of the pole and hauling himself in by means of a hook. Pregnant at the time she promptly fainted! Vic was a man of impulse and apparently it was no great surprise to his wife that he should take on such a feat but she had certainly not been forewarned.

Mr Roe made sure Vic was kept suitably fed and watered by sending up regular meals on a tray hoisted into the barrel by rope. Any 'waste products' were returned in a suitable container to the ground using the same principle.

Conditions in the barrel were cramped to say the least and at one point Mr Reeves felt the need to contact a masseur by telephone to seek advice for swollen ankles and sore feet. All this, of course, from the barrel. The weather was not always favourable, either. A thunderstorm caused the barrel to twist and swing alarmingly and on other days the heat was hard to bear. Passing double decker buses often got a wave – the people on the top deck could see him quite clearly – and it is said that Vic respectfully removed the handkerchief protecting his head from the heat when a hearse passed by. He did not return to the safety of the ground for thirty-one and a half days from 19 July to 19 August 1952, earning himself a well-deserved place in the *Guinness Book of Records*. During that time Vic became a major tourist attraction, coaches would bring people to Walsall to see the man in the barrel and news spread across the country as people followed his world record attempt.

Mr Roe enjoyed the publicity for his restaurant and Mr Reeves won his wager, the amount of which he never disclosed.

Mr Reeves died in 2001 of stomach cancer. He never lost his sense of fun despite years of failing health. He had done many jobs throughout the years, but his main one was as a lumberjack, which took him all over the country. He was a man who enjoyed travelling.

Already in his later years he once went to Rome. Armed only with a walking stick he found one way to deal with Italian drivers – holding his stick out in front of him and stopping the traffic by marching out into the road undaunted. During the same trip he spotted an unusual shaped bottle, to which his wife took a fancy and he bought it for her as a present. On examination on the plane home it became clear that it was in fact mineral water bottled in Wales!

Vic's spirit of adventure and love of fun live on through his daughter, Vicky Reeves. She took part in a sponsored piano push from Walsall to Wales in 1983 spanning two full days and raising £6,500 for muscular dystrophy. The push was done in relays but she was there throughout. She would very much like to take on a challenge now but illness makes this difficult and, of course, in earlier years girls were discouraged from such 'foolhardiness'.

Vicky Reeves

My great-great-great grandfather, Benjamin Dean

Mary Ann Couzens, wife of Ben Dean, in 1882 aged forty.

Benjamin Dean was born at Daw End in the parish of Rushall, Staffordshire, on the 3 July 1839 to a typical working class family. Ben had seven older siblings – four sisters and three brothers. Benjamin's father, William, was a limestone miner and his mother, Jane, was the daughter of Samuel and Frances Nuttall who had come from Dudley, another limestone mining area, presumably to find work. Ben was born at a time when children had to go to work early, and there were few opportunities for education and he was no exception. Like most working class children, Ben didn't have much of a chance to get an education at school and probably only attended about twelve times.

At about ten years old, Ben went to work at the Daw End lime pits and then, as a teenager, went on to ob tain similar work near Wednesbury, walking to and from his employment every day (a distance of some five miles each way!). Ben would have been working from ten to twelve hours each day.

Sadly, at the age of about twelve, his father died and from that time and for years afterwards the petty wages of the young boy, and then the young man, contributed to the support of his mother and siblings. Until he

Mary Ann Couzens aged about ninety.

was about twenty, Benjamin was content to live much the same, unmotivated life as his young peers of the time because his culture and background brought him up to be a miner, and this is the life and job everybody around him was accustomed to. With their minimal education and a working class background, Ben's three brothers were happy to accept a future in the mining industry, as generations before them had, and didn't think once about trying to educate themselves. However, Ben's view of life was soon to change.

The person who opened Ben's eyes to the advantages of education was a servant girl called Mary Ann Couzens (born in Somerset 1842, died 1935). Ben met this lady in the 1850s and she was to influence his life in a way that he could not have anticipated. Ben fell in love with Mary and asked her to marry him, however she refused and it was this heart-breaking refusal that was to veer him in the direction of great success and determination. She would not consent to marriage unless he fulfilled two conditions. Firstly he must stop drinking and secondly he must learn to write his name. He must have abided by these two strictures because on the 3 August 1863 they were married at Wednesbury parish church and his signature was clear to see on the certificate.

As a married man of twenty-four, Mary helped him to realize the advantages of an education and, in spite of every adverse circumstance, he educated himself and rapidly rose in the estimation of his fellow workmen. It is not known exactly how Ben found the time for an education whilst working a day of around twelve hours, however, with a lot of determination and the help of his wife and brother-in-law, Samuel Couzens, slowly Ben's literacy blossomed.

As well as Mary Ann, the 'Self Help' book by Samuel Smiles, published in 1859 is also thought to have motivated Ben and widened his view on education. The 'Self Help' book was aimed at the working class to enforce the idea that nothing creditable can be accomplished without application and diligence and that the student must not be daunted by difficulties, but conquer them by patience and perseverance and, above all, must seek elevation of character.

In 1871, soon after Ben married Mary Ann, they moved homes to live at No. 97, Mill Lane, Butts (then a newly developed part of Rushall Parish). It was probably at this time that he started taking an interest in the nascent trade union movement and also local affairs. Mary Ann and Ben now had two children, William (1871-1958) and Samuel.

When Ben moved to Mill Lane he became a registered voter. This was four years after the Representation of the People Act was passed in 1867. The act increased the number of people who could vote from 813,000 (nation-wide) to 2 million, however, it didn't alter the age at which you were allowed to vote which remained at twenty-one and women were still not entitled. You could only vote if you owned property worth at least £10 (if rented), so Benjamin was clearly rising in status.

Although Ben now had the sought after qualities of a literate man, he was certainly not well off. His paid positions in the Miner's Union now made him slightly better off than if he had remained a working miner and his financial status now made it possible for him to participate in local affairs as a Town Councillor. At the time councillors and aldermen were unpaid, they did not even receive expenses to compensate for loss of earnings. Ben's job as secretary of the Pelsall miners would have been much more pleasant than working down the cramped, dusty mines with just the flickering light of a candle to guide his twelve hours work.

Ben's first known public office was in February 1887 when he became vice-chairman of Rushall School Board. This voluntary position shows that Ben was now

This certificate recorded Ben Dean's position as treasurer of The Midland Miner's Federation.

becoming confident in his new found literacy and wanted to promote its benefits to the residents of the village in which he lived. The first known evidence of his political beliefs also appeared in 1887 when he became a member of the Walsall Radical Club. The most important event was the formation of the Cannock Chase Miners' Union and also the Walsall branch of the National Mineworkers, both as part of the Midland Miner's Federation of which he became honorary treasurer.

New doors were opening in Ben's life now he was a totally literate man. In 1888 he became Secretary of Walsall Radical Club and formed the Pelsall Miner's Union, of which he remained secretary until his death. In this year of great activity he also became a member of Bridge Ward (Walsall) branch of the Liberal Club. This was a position to be retained until the following year when he resigned both from this and as secretary of the Radical Club. In 1890 he joined the Hatherton Ward Liberal Association Committee, and was chosen by Bridge Ward as their candidate for the forthcoming elections to Walsall Town Council. Probably one of the most important events that happened in his life was being elected as Ward Councillor on the 1 November 1890. He was the first working class man ever to be elected to Walsall Council and one of the first in the country.

When Ben joined the council he became a member of the following committees: Gas Undertaking, Parks and Sewage Farm and Health, so joining the small group of leading citizens of the town who were to bring Walsall slowly into the twentieth century. Most of the Council members were well-to-do solicitors, factory and mine owners, shopkeepers etc. The sort of people a decade previously who Ben could have been working for, but now he was playing an important role as the only direct representative of the working class.

The following year there were further elections and this time he was elected member for Birchill's Ward, and in addition to his existing responsibilities also became a member of the Watch committee, which employed the local police force and ran the magistrate's court. Adding to his many roles, he also became an executive of the National Miner's Union and a member of the recently formed Walsall Trades Council. At this stage in his life and right up until his death Ben was truly devoted to the people of Walsall and his dedicated work spanned many years. During the year of 1891 he also managed to find time to become a member of a committee formed to try and open a Liberal Club in Walsall, an aim which was achieved on 29 December of that year.

Another huge thing that Ben accomplished was to become the first working class man ever to be appointed as a Magistrate (Justice of the Peace) to the Walsall Bench, on the 23 May 1893.

Ben also played a major part in the settlement of a great strike in the coal mining industry, which commenced in July when the owners tried to impose a 25% reduction in wages. This was his first major involvement in a dispute that had more than local importance (there were to be many more) and as you can imagine he had very strong views on the subject, being a former miner himself. Ben was renowned for his fair and unbiased opinion, neither for nor against any social class. His views on strikes were expressed in his obituary in the *Walsall Observer* of the 12 March 1910: 'Mr Dean hated strikes and never resorted to their use until all other methods had failed and amicable settlements were beyond the bounds of attainment'. Ben was said to be very good at finding compromises in disputes.

A measure of the respect and esteem in which he was now held was shown when he was re-elected unopposed as Councillor for Birchills Ward. He was now a member of at

Ben Dean's house in Borneo Street, as it is today.

least nine other committees and organizations and must have found it very hard to find time for all his activities.

In 1898 there was a major strike in the Welsh Mining Town of Abertillery and Ben was sent for to act as mediator between the miners and the owners. The result seems to have been satisfactory for the local miners as they presented him with a gold watch fob, inscribed 'Presented to Alderman W. Dean, JP in recognition of services rendered to Wales during their struggle in 1898 by his Abertillery friends'.

The strike resulted in a sliding scale of payment and a request for a 10% wage increase. It lasted from April to August and ended in a return to the status quo that had existed before the dispute began. During this year Ben was elected to the Miner's Federation of Great Britain, as he had been in 1892, 1893 and 1895.

Ben's various committee positions changed as the years progressed and he also represented the Council as a governor of Queen Mary's Schools (Mayfield and the boy's and girl's grammar schools).

Benjamin had a house built at 57, Borneo Street, where he was to live until his death. On Sunday nights, Ben is said to have opened house to everyone and anyone was invited to discuss the topics of the day. People from all classes and backgrounds would gather together, their occupations ranging widely: miners, labourers, solicitors, accountants, teachers etc. Among his close friends were W.H. Duignan (historian and solicitor) and 'Lawyer' Jackson. Most Friday nights Ben also organized an open-air political meeting on Pelsall Common on the Wolverhampton Road. After the meeting they would all go down to the pub, then called 'The Miner's Arms' but Ben drank little, if at all.

Whilst Ben was living in Borneo Street many of the leading radical men of the day stayed there, including Stephen Walsh MP, William Brace (1865-1947) from Monmouthshire and Enoch Edwards MP (1852-1912) who was also 2nd President of the Miner's Federation of Great Britain.

In 1900 he became a trustee of the Pelsall Mining Disaster Fund, which had been established in 1873. Also in this year his business acquired an address Park Street for use as a retail shop. This was a very small shop and used as a retail tobacconist until the 1960s. He also bought a shop at 105 Lichfield Street, which remained in the family's possession until the 1950s. My grandfather, also called William Dean, served behind the counter of this shop as a teenager around 1979 and met many customers who remembered Ben.

Another landmark for Ben and Walsall came in 1901 when he was elected Alderman

Ben Dean held political meetings in this Pelsall pub. In those days it was called The Miner's Arms.

Ben Dean, Mayor of Walsall, 1906.

Ben Dean's family.

The Dean family taken in about 1882.

for Birchills in place of the local iron master, James Lindop. Again he was the first working class man to fill this office. The following year, Ben's position as Alderman was changed from Birchills to Alderman for Caldmore Ward and his busy life became even busier because he was now also Chairman of the Cemeteries Committee.

The next few years of Benjamin's life passed without any great change until Friday 8 November 1906 when he was unanimously elected Mayor of Walsall. Again Ben was the first working class man to fill this position and he may have been the first working class mayor in Britain.

Ben had five sons and four daughters: Frederick, Wilfred, William, Arthur, Samuel, Sarah, Emily, Elizabeth and Mary. Although Ben had a very busy working and social life he loved his family dearly, and whilst struggling to make the world a happier place he didn't forget them. Ben's feelings towards his large family are described in his obituary: 'Nothing was so sacred and religious to him as his family life'. Ben certainly helped William, Samuel and Wilfred to earn some money by building the tobacconist and hardware businesses, which benefited many generations of the Dean family right up until the 1960s when my grandfather and his brother sold it.

The triumphs and achievements that Ben had during his life were a great inspiration to many, including his family. William followed in his father's footsteps by becoming a councillor at Walsall Town Council, then an alderman and later the Mayor (1932-1933). William also showed great dedication to the Liberal Party throughout his life as Ben had done for over a quarter of a century. Like Benjamin, Frederick became Secretary of the Pelsall Miner's Union as well as working as a miner.

Both Fred and Wilfred became JPs. Arthur's son and daughter both became JPs and William's grandson (my grandfather) followed the family's footsteps and also became a

Ben Dean's tombstone at Rygate Cemetery, Walsall.

councillor. Three of Benjamin's children went on to own successful businesses.

All of Ben's children lived completely different lives to that of their father due to the fact that they had not been born into a poor, mining family, as he had. Although people's views in general had changed and technology had developed, the only real reason why the lives of two generations of one family, born only a quarter of a century apart, were so different was because of Ben's determination to achieve and succeed in life.

During the course of his life Ben had seen many changes in the way people viewed the working class. I think that he would have passed his lifetime experiences on to his children because he wanted to teach people that those in lower social classes had just as much right to be listened to as those higher up. Ben's teachings would have helped them to be as fair-minded and righteous as their father had been.

Summarized from a history project by Rachael Sheldon, aged fourteen

My Gran

Prize-winning entry

In the early 1800s Joseph Severn worked as a wheelwright. His son David became a blacksmith. On 28 June 1847, David married Elizabeth Hodgson at the Collegiate Church in Wolverhampton. They had five children: John, Jane, Ann, Henry and Mary who were all baptized at St Lawrence church, Darlaston, between 1849 and 1860.

The eldest daughter, Jane, met Arthur Rose who, in 1881, lived at Goldthorn Court, Goldthorn Road, Moseley. When they married Jane was disowned by her family because she married Arthur who was a mere chain-maker working in an iron works.

Arthur and Jane had six children – Arthur, David, Joseph, Rosannah, Lily and George. Arthur Snr worked at Noah Hingley's iron works in Netherton, Dudley, along with his son Arthur Jnr, Joseph and George. They helped to make the anchor chain for the *Titanic* in 1911. David went into farming in Wales. Lily married a man named Mr Tibbets who owned a barber's shop.

Rosannah was my gran. She was born in 1885. In 1903, at the age of eighteen, she married a man named Alfred Russell who was a widower with three growing girls. My gran and Alfred had a daughter, Aldyth Vera May, born in 1905. They were living at that time at 321/2 Newhall Street in Walsall.

In 1910 my gran lived at 42 Longacre Street with a Mr William Hill. He was a Hansom Cab driver, stationed in Station Street, Walsall. When Irish immigrants got off the train in Walsall, if they had nowhere to stay the night

My gran Rosannah (date unknown).

Mr Hill would take them back to his house, tip the children out of their beds and let the immigrants have a bed for the night. On a Saturday night he would often take home a leading dignitary of Walsall, after dropping off his customer's lady friend, and was well tipped for keeping quiet about his fares.

On 24 June 1910 their son William Alfred was born. He was my father. Although William Alfred was the son of William Hill, he took the name Russell because gran was still married to Alfred Russell, who by this time had left her and gone to live with his eldest daughter, Kit, in Smethwick.

In 1926 the family lived at 31 Day Street, Walsall. Aldyth married Harold Holford on 5 April of that year.

By 1933 my gran and William Hill were married and living at 132 Miner Street in the Birchills. On 15 October 1933 my father William married Susan Cope of Block 73

Chainmakers working at Noah Higley's Ironworks in 1911. This is the anchor chain for the Titanic, *which Arthur Rose and his sons helped to make.*

Rosannah Rose, aged eighteen, taken before her marriage to Alfred Russell in 1903.

Green Lane, Walsall, at St Patrick's Church, Blue Lane. They were going to live with my gran and Mr Hill in Miner Street, but on the day that they married and moved in, my gran packed her bags and moved out, leaving Mr Hill for my parents to look after. She went to be a housekeeper for a doctor who lived on the Birmingham Road in Walsall.

'Granddad' Hill was a stickler for everything to be done his way. There was only one easy chair in the house and he had to have it. If you had jam on your bread you were not allowed butter and he was very adept with his walking stick. One word from us children and we felt the crack of it. He certainly believed in children being seen and not heard, but, for all that, he was a dear old man.

Mr Hill died in 1944, and by this time gran was living in Farm Street, Hockley, Birmingham, in a back-to-back house, where she lived with a man called Albert Jaggers. These back houses were three stories high with just one room on the ground floor, one bedroom above and an attic room above that. There were two small brew-houses, which everyone on the yard used to wash dishes, wash clothes and wash themselves. There were two evil-smelling lavatories which dozens of people used. Some of these houses had numerous families living in them. Sometimes a whole large family would live in one room.

In 1944, after Mr Hill died, Gran married Albert Jaggers and they moved into a sweet shop, which was at the front of their back-to-back house. This shop was just one room. You walked into the shop and behind a board on the left all the sweets were spread out in boxes in the window. There was a curtain across the room and behind the curtain was a table on which stood the scales etc. The curtain was open about two feet wide, but when gran weighed the sweets she did so behind the curtain out of sight of the customers.

As you stood at the table serving the customers behind you was a large black range with an open fire, which I had to black-lead when I went over. At one side of the range was a box with a cushion on it, which was all there was to sit on, and at the other side of the grate was an old gas cooker on which gran cooked food to sell to the customers, mostly the Lucas factory workers.

The workers would pop into the shop, order what they wanted and then go back for their order at lunchtime. Gran also cooked jacket potatoes and peas, which she would wrap in a little square of paper and sell for a penny. Opposite the shop door was a small cubicle behind another curtain where there was a sink, a cold water tap and also a door

William Hill (Front right).

Hansom cab drivers. William Hill is standing on the left.

which opened inwards revealing steps down to the cellar. Next to the cooker there was a door leading up to the bedroom and above that was the attic. There was no lavatory in the place. You had to go into the street and up the entry to the two lavatories in the yard.

Gran was a formidable lady. We were always terrified of her as children. Dad would take us to see her and she never gave us one sweet. When I was old enough I used to go and stay with her during weekends and holidays. After lunch she would shut up shop and go to bed for an hour for a rest. I would sit on the box in the shop thinking, 'Dare I take one?'. I never dared. Gran always said that she had counted them all and I didn't doubt her. I was afraid of her even though she was asleep.

I have no idea when Albert Jaggers died, but I can only ever remember gran being at the shop on her own, although she did have another 'gentleman' who would take her for a drink in the Brummagum Arms. He was a Jewish man who made jewellery in his house. He once made me a beautiful necklace and a bracelet made with real silver threepenny bits. This gentleman must have been one of the original jewellery makers who started the jewellery quarter in Birmingham.

In 1956 gran was burgled and knocked about badly. Two boys one night prised up the cellar grid in the street, got down into the cellar, came up into the shop, and pocketed lots of cigarettes. Then they went up into the bedroom and beat up gran to make her give them the shops takings, all her money and her jewellery.

These boys had pillow cases over their heads, but gran recognized their voices. They were caught with all the things they had taken. Gran had to give the shop up after this and she came back to Walsall to live with her daughter Aldyth.

Sadly Gran went senile and ended her days in

Gran Rosannah Jaggers at my wedding on 12 June 1958.

William Hill and dog, Jack, in the garden in Moat Road, Walsall.

Beacon lodge, in Pleck Road, Walsall, where she died on the 21 August 1960, aged seventy-five. This was a very sad end to a lady who had lived a very interesting life. Maybe she hadn't lived her life as she should have done, but she certainly must have had guts to do what she did, and live her life the way she wanted to live it.

As a man who knew her once said in a radio interview – you couldn't forget Mrs Jaggers – once known, never forgotten.

Pauline Brown

Some recollections of my Grannie Nicklin

Grannie Nicklin – the use of her Christian name would have been improper – was not your typical cuddly old dear with a bun. She was a determined, generous but self-centred lady with a widow's hump who did nothing by halves. She liked to please and would give to excess, but most of all she liked to have her own way.

How I wish I had known her in her younger days: her parties, her extravagant dresses and her flamboyant lifestyle. Apparently she even smoked! But I could not view her in the past, only see her in her later years. When I was ten, she was in her late sixties and still trying, despite her arthritis, to play tennis with my brother, David, and me. She would like to take us out on the bus to various interesting places such as Sutton Park and we would ride on the top deck. She would insist on struggling up the stairs to get the best view.

Occasionally, we would stay with her overnight on her feather bed and enjoy breakfast the next morning snuggled down in comfort. Breakfast in bed: luxury! 'Don't tell your Mum.', she would say.

I was impressed with her ability to put a whole cream cracker biscuit in her mouth and eat it without losing a crumb. But even more unbelievable to me, I would catch her licking her nose with her long tongue, but try as I might; I couldn't manage it.

Poor Grannie we did play her up! We would ask her, 'If frozen water is iced water. What is frozen ink?' She always answered 'I stink!' Did we catch her out each time or did she know her response would create a laugh? I shall never know.

Grannie was born on New Years Day 1885 and called Esther Mary Lillie Harvey. What a striking name: no-one else in the family had three first names, but I only ever heard her called Ettie. Although she was born in Belvedere Road near the Matthew Harvey factory where her father had his business, the family soon moved to Brackenwood, a spacious house on the Birmingham Road, Great Barr opposite the Bell Inn. She was the eldest of five, excluding Fredrick Kenneth, her brother who died before he reached the age of two. Her three sisters and a brother were Hilda Grace, Mildred known as Sissie, Marion and Sydney and she out lived all of them. At Brackenwood, she was brought up with tennis courts, a croquet lawn, servants and plenty of space to play games. Even so, Grannie would tell us how, during a cold winter, she would have to break the ice in the water jug before she could pour it out for her early morning wash. This did not lessen her affection for her former home.

Always a lady, she had to have silk next to her skin, so as silk combinations were not on sale in Walsall, she sent away for them. I could not understand how she got into her 'comms', as she called them, they looked far too complicated. Fancy having your vest and knickers all in one! 'They would make things difficult in the smallest room', I thought. She also liked to wear green and I can't remember seeing her in any other colour.

On alternate Sundays our family would visit Grannie Nicklin for our tea when we enjoyed 'ham and cream cakes'. She discovered that one of our favourite meals was ham salad followed by those wonderful, huge, soft meringues held together with thick cream. As she wanted to impress, that is what we had at each meal and so the family joke of 'ham and cream cakes' was born. Grannie loved to give us boxes of chocolates – I always had 'Black Magic' and when I offered her one she would take a soft centre wrongly thinking I preferred the hard ones.

As she grew older, she found new ways of getting out and about. So when the mood took her, or with the arrangement of her friend Emmeline Eyland, she would ring for a taxi. She used a man named 'Swinbourne' to request a trip to Wales for the day. They would go and have lunch at a nice hotel and return for the evening. Alternatively, they would use Mr Ponter, the taxi man preferred by Miss Eyland. The drivers did quite well out of it as they would have a meal on top of the fee for the day and the ladies would compete over who gave the largest tip.

Beside her favourite taxi driver, Grannie had an odd job man whom she would summon to do all manner of work around the house: putting up new curtain rails, moving large pieces of furniture or undertaking minor repairs. She always called him 'Pennel'. He could be seen sweating and puffing trying to keep up with her demands – poor man!

Never satisfied with the place where she was living, she moved house frequently but always remained in Walsall. I remember her owning three (or was it four?) different houses on Sutton Road and then she moved to 176 Birmingham Road, a house where she had lived previously. The wonderful Mr Pennel was always around to assist.

It was at this last house that I realised how determined she was to get what she wanted. When her bed was moved downstairs and she lived in what was previously the lounge, she had the telephone transferred to her bedside. From there, one day, she called for the taxi and I was told to open the front door so that Mr Swinbourne could come in. Sworn to secrecy, I waited and when he arrived, she asked him to fetch a bottle of brandy for her and gave him a note. He returned with the goods and was also made to promise not to tell.

Grannie had difficulty in sleeping and so drank brandy along with her sleeping pills. My dad, Kenneth, had forbidden her to have alcohol while she was taking barbiturates but she wanted it, so she found a way to get it. Every night she took four pink Soneryl with a swig of brandy, which worked quite well for a short while but she would wake in the dark of the night. This was the time she drank liquid Paraldehyde. I was fascinated by the clear liquid which froze in the bottle on a cold night and which had such a strong ether-like smell that I didn't know how anyone could touch it. One gulp and she was asleep again. However, her whole being oozed the fumes of Paraldehyde on the following morning. It is as well that her midnight knockout is no longer available.

As she sat in bed, she liked to look at the what was happening along Birmingham Road so her dressing table mirror had to be tilted to just the right angle for her to view the footpath and neighbour's gardens.

Unfortunately, the window frame was so high that however the mirror was adjusted she thought she was missing some of the action. Her answer was to have the window removed together with the lower two rows of bricks so a new, larger frame could be inserted. What determination!

This obstinate streak was at the heart of her frequent rows with my dad: her only child. She spent money without consideration of the consequences and Dad was convinced that she would run out of her inheritance and end up destitute. He would return home worried and she would continue, as before, to use whatever money was available. She had the view that when it had gone, something else would turn up.

'What happened to Grandpa?' you may ask.

Ellie Nicklin.

Geoffrey Nicklin married his Ettie on 31 July 1911 at the Particular Baptist Chapel in Midland Road, Walsall. By the time I had arrived on the scene, the family did not speak about him and questions were generally left unanswered but Grannie did tell me that he was a coalman. A coalman marrying a well-off young lady! Really? Grandpa was a leather merchant, the marriage certificate states. Well! The story seems to be that the business ran into difficulty financially and he ended up penniless. However, his name does not appear in any of the contemporary London Gazzettes, which record the names of bankrupts. Rumour also has it that Geoffrey was found behind a locked door with his secretary. Was it an indiscretion, the failure of his business or the over spending habits of his wife that led to his problems? Whichever was the cause, the result was that Geoffrey was banished, it seems, from Walsall. He went to live in Erdington, where he did deliver coal and where he died in 1949.

Grannie must have been lonely during her last few years, so she took a paid companion, Miss Richards. They spent many hours playing the board game 'Sorry' and her long-suffering companion hated it. I often wondered if there was any significance in this! I don't think so. I am sure she chose to play this game, as she knew she could beat her opponent.

Finally, Grannie died aged eighty-three on 18 August 1968 but her memory still lives with me. Aggravating she was at times, but never boring and how I loved her! I hope my grandchildren think as much of me, as I did of her.

Anne James

Walsall's last official town crier?

'Walsall has never had a town crier'. Such was the general comment I received whenever I raised the topic with local politicians in the 1980s and 1990s. In 1988, I made myself a town crier's outfit, but found the need for a crier had been cancelled. Yet I had been carrying out the function in a number of situations and felt it was about time that I knew a little bit more about the history of such an activity, preferably in the town that I had made a family home since the early 1960s.

It would seem sensible to go back a few centuries so that we can find out what a town crier was and what the functions of such a job were. But there's the rub; not only is it very difficult to find anything written on the subject, but it is also very unusual to find any mention of this 'official' in anything other than a passing reference of the need for one or in such written items as 'or fleeing from justice after a hue and cry has been raised' (extract from *Historical Collections*, Staffordshire, vol. 3, p 18). As good a place to start as any is the written charters that emerged from the rulers in the centuries following the invasion of William I from Normandy in 1066.

The difficulty in Walsall, which according to tradition is a 'Borough by Prescription', is to find an existing charter earlier than 1627 (Charles I). I understand that the extant one is a charter issued by Charles II in the 1660s and, even had I seen it, I would have found it difficult to read in its natural form. When Charles II issued this to the Mayor and Burgesses of the town, it was a charter defining exactly what privileges he was granting to the town. However, it did not make completely clear how this fitted in with the structure of the manorial system controlled by the lord of the manor. Neither did this make clear how this fitted in with being a 'Borough of Prescription', that is one which has been in existence since time immemorial.

However, by the mid-seventeenth century many of the towns throughout the country were boroughs in their own right, as outlined by Sidney and Beatrice Webb in their book

Even then it rained sometimes!

The Manor and the Borough, first published in 1908. It is also stated in a letter to a colleague in historical correspondence in Walsall archives that, after Stafford and Burton-on-Trent, Walsall was probably the oldest Borough Corporation in the country. So how does Henry Griffin fit into all this? First I think I ought to explain what a borough corporation is.

Whilst the tendency is to think of kings and queens ruling the country from London, the reality was that authority had to be delegated to wealthy and influential people in the provinces. Taxes and other forms of income also had to be collected. As good a way as any of doing this was to allow certain people, generally supported by their own wealth or the collective wealth of a group e.g. a guild in that area, to control activities in that locality by granting a charter (a license) usually for a fee.

There were, of course, many restrictions and provisos to ensure that the king did not give away too much (shades of the Magna Carta?), but the charter was usually addressed to the Mayor and the Capital Burgesses of the town often with other officials defined, for example the Recorder, to ensure that special legal activities were or were not carried out. The number and the titles of officials varied from city to city and town to town. In Walsall, according to the charter, control was given to the Mayor, twenty-four Burgesses, a Recorder, a Town Clerk and two Sergeants-at-Mace. The Mayor was almost invariably the chief magistrate, which usually was an unpaid post only held by virtue of an individual's personal wealth.

The variability of appointments and offices thus presents a difficulty, along with a lack of written evidence, in deciding whether, over the early centuries, the offices of Town Crier, Bellman or Beadle, (or whichever title was used for the person who acted as a messenger for the mayor), in Walsall were separate or not.

The Sergeants-at-Mace are mentioned continually in the mayoral accounts from 1595. In the records kept in Walsall Local History Centre in Essex Street, but with little supporting evidence available, it is impossible to define if or how a Sergeant-at-Mace could be involved with town crying activities. From 1595 to the early nineteenth century, the mayor's accounts invariably show the mayoral allowance per annum (£10 for over a century) always followed by an amount for a cloak for the Sergeant-at-Mace. This cloak was obviously a symbol of office. Were there two of them? Was one seen as senior since he was also engaged in town crying activities in the early seventeenth century and did he get additional remuneration as did Henry Griffin, shown in the census of 1881, as Town Crier, aged seventy-five?

As can be seen from the copy of the minutes of the Borough Council of the 1 April 1850 (April fool jokers, please note that the meeting was held after noon – in the evening in fact), the two posts were linked. Apart from the various council minutes in the ensuing thirty years or so – Henry to have a new coat or to fight for a new pair of breeches – the intriguing aspect for me is why was Henry appointed at all? For the two Sergeants-at-Mace in 1835, one being Henry Wainwright, a butcher, had been in office and Town Crier from 1835 until early 1850. It is not clear why he resigned. Also unclear is why his name was on the short list of applicants for the post being refilled in that April and one wonders at the 'shenanigans' going on in local government even then. Mind you, there had been a Corporation Act in 1835 which made great upheavals in local government throughout the country, so who knows? Was Henry Wainwright appointed following the Improvement Acts of the 1820s, similar to the Walsall Improvement and Markets Act of 1848, which ultimately led to a new Guild Hall on Goodall Street? Or was he a victim of political in-fighting? Could it be that Henry Griffin really was an old boy of Queen Mary's Grammar School; that someone better educated was needed to win the preferred post as a last dying gesture of the old Capital Burgesses in defiance of the 'Modernists' who wanted more efficiency? Or was it jobs for the boys?

So what about Henry Griffin? What happened to him? Apart from being a harness plater in 1841, a baker in 1845, a provision dealer in 1851/1861 and a clothes dealer in 1865 he is listed in Kelly's Directory of 1870 amongst the Corporation persons as 'Town Crier and Sergeant-at-Mace' Other than this we do not know a great deal.

The earliest date readable in the mayor's accounts is from 1637, when Thomas Wollaston paid the sergeants £4 for their wages. The last mention of Henry Griffin could be said to be in the *Walsall Observer and South Staffordshire Chronicle*, Saturday 8 December 1888, when a good four inches of column was used for his eulogy. He was reported as being aged eighty-three.

From other private sources it is known that he lived on Upper Rushall Street and that his wife, Maria, ran a baker's and confectioner's shop from there. Also there is information showing that, while he seemed to welcome the Mormons when they visited the town in the 1850s, (it is thought that he welcomed them into his home) he evidently became unhappy about their influence on his wife. The end result was that his wife, Maria, ultimately left to make the long journey to

Wednesday, Janu

Vieira pledge on his future

Arsenal captain

with
m Nash

have their say on another
rating Molineux season

irt logo can
y conjure
crispier

Utah, USA, with their daughters following. Henry still carried on his duties in Walsall, living in Newport Street in 1881 with a housekeeper twenty years his junior. She was probably needed, as he was sufficiently ill for the Council to pay him his wages for a considerable time, even though he was unable to carry out his duties.

Because of the way his appointment was seen (and paid) as the senior of the two Sergeants-at-Mace and because of his obvious strength of personality and character, which obliged him to still define himself as a Town Crier in the census of 1881, I am quite sure he is the Sergeant-at-Mace prominently shown on the painting on display in the Flint Gallery in Lichfield Street entitled 'Walking the Fair' and painted in 1857.

Following the newspaper report in 1888 there appear to be no further records of the appointment of another Sergeant-at-Mace, who was also a Town Crier. Later many were recruited from the retiring policemen. The Police Force had developed quite dramatically from the 'Bobbys' of the 1830s and 1840s.

Where does this leave us?

It leaves me with the need for more research and the desire to see the re-instatement of this old office, not just in Walsall or even the present day, but in all or most of the ancient boroughs (and even new ones) in Great Britain, to keep our historical heritage alive, as well as adding a little more colour to the day.

Cyril Richardson

Sister Dora
To Worship and To Serve: Was Sister Dora a stereotypical nineteenth-century woman or a feminist hero?

Sister Dora (1832–1878) holds almost iconic status in Walsall. Her contribution to nursing in the locality has been eulogised by historians and her popularity publicly marked by a statue being erected to her (the first in England to a woman other than royalty) and a hospital, a road, a nurse's cap and even an LNW railway engine named after her. Her public life exists through narrative accounts and it is easy to slip into hagiography. Indeed, Chris Latimer, of Walsall Local History Centre, calls her 'the most remarkable person in Walsall's history.'

However, although some of Sister Dora's letters remain, her first biographer in 1881, Margaret Lonsdale, concealed names and dates to protect reputations, so the lack of 'pure' primary evidence prevents deeper insight into her true character.

Even a cursory glance through the archives suggests difficulties with examining traditional historical lines of enquiry to discover whether or not her local work was representative of national nursing or whether her success had an effect on other women locally. However, closer inspection of the life of the venerable Sister Dora raises more questions than it answers. I wanted to probe further, to look at the woman rather than the myth. There are tantalising glimpses of unconventionality, mere hints of personality transcendent of the projected view of staid, respectable Victorian womanhood which all led to one fascinating question: Is Sister Dora a stereotypical nineteenth-century woman – submissive, passive and weak – or a feminist hero – strong-willed, pioneering and independent? In order to answer this question, one must start by taking into account family and religious influences upon the young Dorothy.

Dorothy Pattison was born at Hauxwell Rectory in Wensleydale into an enclosed and claustrophobic environment, which compelled rather than deterred her. Her father, Reverend Mark Pattison, was obsessed with enforcing his authority over his wife and daughters. Her father and mother, Jane, were strictly Evangelical, a regime which emphasised obedience and duty and encouraged self-denial and submission as primary virtues. Her mother's belief in the absolute obedience of a wife to her husband never wavered. Even when her husband raged and grew violent towards her, when he refused to let her see her married children and forbade his daughters to carry out charity work, she remained submissive and urged her children to do likewise. This can be perceived later in Dorothy's philosophy of nursing, by putting others before herself. The more arduous her service to other people, the less she could reproach herself for selfishness or self-indulgence. This most formative influence on Dorothy's ideas can be traced throughout her life.

Religious education was, therefore, an important part of her life. Her brother, Mark, joined the Oxford Movement, the new spirit in English Christianity, a realisation that the poor of Victorian England were being neglected both physically and spiritually by the Church. Dorothy embraced this movement ardently in the face of her father's fierce opposition, not being afraid of hostility. She regarded her later work as a duty to God and believed that the successful treatment of patients was a manifestation through her hands of the power of God's love.

Dorothy did not like the traditional lessons meted out to young girls, 'I didn't want to be a fine drawing room lady, but a nurse. I was sure I shouldn't want them in this world or the next.'

With the £90 she was left by her mother on her death, Dorothy, then aged twenty-nine, left the family home in Yorkshire and, after a brief spell as a schoolmistress, she joined the Christ Church Sisterhood near Middlesborough, which was devoted to religious observance and charitable work. The Sisterhood offered a chance to combine the most important influences in her life, namely to worship and to serve. Her ambition to become a nurse, inspired by the work of Florence Nightingale (who, ironically, declined the invitation to unveil the statue of Sister Dora), was realised when novice Dora, as she was now known, was sent to the Cottage Hospital in Walsall in 1865, due to a staffing crisis.

It was in Walsall:

...a rough and tough town without hospital and shocking industrial accidents, with little or no provision for safety or medical care; overpopulation with no housing provision, the dwellings... a breeding ground for disease...

that Sister Dora was to establish her reputation and to spend the rest of her life. Ten years later, she finally resigned from the Sisterhood to concentrate on her nursing. One can only speculate on how her noviciate affected her attitudes towards duty and work but all of these influences can be said to have played an important part in her life and be the cause of the complexity and dichotomy of her character. Hers can be seen as a lonely and relentless life, lacking the usual trappings and social expectations of a comfortable middle-class existence.

Concerning the issue of marriage in Sister Dora's life, came the questions:

Could I love him well enough to give him my future; a future in which I can but live for others? Would it be selfishness or unselfishness to love one instead of many? Am I needed elsewhere? Are there not other women, noble women at that, who have given up their lives unto the service of charity and therefore God?

Her early failure to marry rested on her

father's domination and his pre-occupation with status – no-one in Hauxwell was considered suitable for even friendship, let alone the contractual binding of two families in matrimony. Later, her dedication to her constant nursing and her Victorian preoccupation with, and confusion about, love and lust, sex and sin would cause her to prevaricate and, ultimately, decide against becoming a wife. Yet she believed very strongly in the virtue of marriage:

If I had to live life over again I would marry, because a woman ought to live with a man and be in subjection.

Though there were no husbands, there were men in her life, perhaps more frequently and more intimately than accords with the stock notion of a mid-Victorian 'saint.' The catalogue of male friendships – the secret affair with a young farmer's son, Purchas Stirke, whilst at the same time being engaged to James Tate, unable to resist both suitors and the subsequent radical breaking of the engagement; the romance with hospital doctor John Redfern Davies and, later, Kenyon Jones of Dudley – might leave the impression that a woman of action had little use for members of her own sex. It is probably true that the dynamic and masterful Miss Pattison lacked sympathy for the average dependent home-bound woman of her generation, although she did have some female friends. Yet it was always her calling that predominated. As a young girl, Dora, talking of the future, had once claimed, 'Oh I'll be a nurse or a lady doctor, and do everything for my patients'.

However, when the opportunity actually arose, she declined. James MacLachlan, new surgeon at the hospital in 1868, tried in vain to persuade her to train as a doctor. She was commended for her skill in setting fractures and in bandaging and doctors valued her opinion on the treatment of all manner of industrial accidents. She attended all post-mortem examinations and dissections in the hospital and even pulled teeth to learn the practice techniques from the doctors. For some time she studied at the Birmingham Ophthalmic Hospital, for she was very interested in the anatomy of the eye, as it was often the subject of accidents in an industrial area. She even visited Paris and London to study new developments in the world of nursing, including new surgical instruments and equipment, and antiseptic surgery under Lister.

However, the inspiration for her career was not medical but religious and to give up nursing for years of study would have run entirely against her beliefs. Had she taken the decision to train as a doctor, however, she would have been a contemporary of Elizabeth Garrett Anderson.

Her conventional religious beliefs can also be seen in her concern for prostitutes, encouraging them to attend services of Evangelists and Methodists. Little is known about her reform work with prostitutes, along with other great contemporaries, because she was reticent to push herself forward: I do not like that kind of thing – ladies speaking in a public room or hall, unless there is really a needs-be'.

Despite her popularity and achievements, the Pattison family never accepted Dora's nursing as a fit occupation for a gentlewoman. Dora's individual nature was aware of opposing attitudes, but she did not heed them for her vocation was all encompassing. Having battled with a series of illnesses throughout her life, she finally succumbed to cancer on Christmas Eve, 1878, aged forty-six, at her cottage in Wednesbury Road, and was awarded a civic funeral before being interred in Queen Street Cemetery. The whole town went into mourning and a muffled peal of the bells of the parish church was rung every evening for a week.

The life of Dorothy Pattison reads like a Victorian novel since she embodied the dichotomy of character of a Charlotte Brontë *Jane Eyre* type figure: submissive on the one hand, the urge to be independent on the other. It was an attitude which her great contemporary, George Eliot, would have understood. Indeed, there are solid grounds for believing that Eliot had heard much about Dorothy from her sister-in-law, Mrs Mark Pattison, who had become an intimate friend of the novelist at the time she was planning *Middlemarch*. Jo Manton, in her biography of Sister Dora, argues convincingly that Dorothea, the heroine of the novel, bears a strong resemblance to Dorothy, even down to the similarity in name. One of the themes of *Middlemarch* is the incompatibility of domesticity and high endeavour, or, in tragic terms, the conflict between love and duty. Sister Dora's life was an illustration of this conflict. Sister Dora, therefore, was an heroic product of Victorian social conditions and Victorian religion and morality. To an extent, she was stereotypical of her generation, but, 'Her restlessness was uncontrollable'.

The battle between early nineteenth century convention and the changing ideologies of the latter nineteenth century are seen to be refracted in the character of Dorothy Pattison: on one hand the angel of mercy doling out comfort and care to the needy and the sick, inspired by a deep religious conviction and an absolute certainty that she was ministering God's holy work on Earth, juxtaposed with the determined woman of independent, though limited, means willing to contravene parental control to lead the life she had chosen.

This strong will also included relationships with the opposite sex: two engagements, both broken off by her, and two romances in later life both concealed, with secret assignations and coded letters. Throughout her life, she put duty and calling above personal desire, making the choice between career and personal happiness, aware that, in Victorian society, these objectives were mutually exclusive.

To approach the life of Sister Dora with modern eyes and to identify her as a feminist is incorrect, for she was inevitably bound by nineteenth century moral and religious ethics, despite what we may read into her behaviour. She did not set out to strike a blow for women, or, necessarily, to set a precedent, but to lead by Christian example a life which had purpose and fulfilment through hard work and devotion to God. That said, though, she still poses enough questions to remain sufficiently and suitably enigmatic to inspire further study. One thing, however, is certain: she is a local legend and as long as her statue stands, she will stay that way.

Lynn Hawthorn

List of Contributors

Vera Astbury
L.G. Banks
Maurice Birch
Pauline Brown
Margaret Cooper
Ted Elwell
Julie Fenton
Mary Giles
Brian Griffiths
D.M. Guy
Jack Haddock
Terry Harrison
Ron Hawkins
Lynn Hawthorn
Terry Henwood
Wendy Hodson
Anne James
Lucy Martin
D. Miller
James Moffat
John Mountford
Lorna Phillips
Leonora Pitt
Vicky Reeves
Cyril Richardson
Tom Rowley
Rachael Sheldon
Ray Slater
Jo Mary Stafford
Kath Taylor
Colin Till
Norman Till
Margo Trubshaw

Shutt Cross House, Walsall Wood Road.